16

Creative
TABLE DECOR
with Indian vegetarian menus

Creative
TABLE DECOR

with Indian vegetarian menus

Nilam Vadera

MERLIN BOOKS

BRAUNTON · DEVON · ENGLAND

ISBN 0 86303 529-9
Printed in England by Maslands Ltd., Tiverton, Devon

FOREWORD

It gives me great pleasure to write a brief foreword to Nilam's book of table design and supporting recipes. Nilam's house parties, some of which I have attended have already come to be regarded as the best of their kind. Two factors, judging from the appreciative comments one has heard repeatedly through the years has commended them to her many guests and these are — the unique way the lunches and dinners are served and the selection of mouth-watering recipes. Careful attention is given to every minor detail. The choice of delicious recipes, colour schemes, and imaginative flower and vegetable decorations are breathtakingly magnificent. The book is full of original and interesting recipes and shows a fascinating approach to serving meals, and I am sure it is guaranteed to impress guests. There is a complete section on napkin arrangement, and new wonderful ways to use flowers and vegetables as well as fruit in table decoration, in the 'Vegetable Floristry' section. I am sure that this book will serve as an invaluable aid to any adventurous hostess for serving meals. I wish Nilam great success for this book which she so richly deserves, and book owners everlasting cooking pleasure.

Lalita Ahmed

INTRODUCTION

A tempting display of creative table designs for entertaining.

Nilam Vadera brings a new concept to the traditions of classic Indian cookery — that of stylish decoration and presentation of vegetarian dishes and sweetmeats, co-ordinating table layout and design with imaginative vegetable floristry.

She draws on wide personal experience of demonstrating Indian cooking to international audiences in East Africa, India, and Great Britain, and of judging culinary competitions. Besides creating exciting new recipes, she has taught the secrets of preparing these gastronomic delights to cooks of both Eastern and Western traditions, vegetarians and non-vegetarians alike.

With this book she would like to share with you the delights of entertaining with delicious and visually enchanting vegetarian food.

A selection of 20 table designs for various occasions are presented spread by spread and illustrated by colour photographs. Each display is accompanied by recipes for the Indian vegetarian dishes and sweetmeats featured, while techniques for achieving the decorative effects are explained in simple terms with the aid of clear illustrations.

Included are tables for: Dinner parties
                              Lunch parties
                              Family celebrations
                              Formal occasions

ACKNOWLEDGEMENTS

This book is a result of many demands and requests from people who have attended my cooking classes and demonstrations to put my ideas on food and table decorations in a concise and easy to follow book. I would like to express my gratitude to all who helped in the preparation of this book.

My sincere thanks also to my mother-in-law, Ramaben Vadera, my daughter-in-law Madhavi and my daughter Shriti for all their help. I would like to thank my husband for his encouragement and support. I would also like to express my gratitude to Kamuben Karia for her support at my cooking classes; to Saloni Thakkar for all her help; to Edward Taylor for all design and artwork; and to Babubhai Shah, of Kenton Photographic Services, for all his suggestions and work. I would also like to thank my family and all the guests of dinner parties for allowing me to test out my cooking ideas on them!

Contents

Cover photograph:
a — Mango Cake
(Brown and Gold
Table p14)
b — A vegetable
flower
arrangement

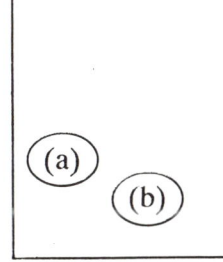

Table Settings

An Introduction to Laying your Table

A beautiful and artistic table arrangement sets the atmosphere for an enjoyable meal. Experimenting with new ideas, colour combinations and methods of presentation is part of the joy of table arrangement. There are no specific rules to follow. Just ask yourself if you like the arrangement you see before you vary it further if you need to. Each persons idea of beauty will vary. A well-decorated table can make the party impressive to your guests and pleasing to yourself.

All the accessories you buy for decorating the table must be chosen with care. They need not be expensive, but must co-ordinate with the rest of the table equipment, i.e. the table-cloth, napkins, cutlery, crockery, glasses, etc. When shopping, spend a little more time exploring and you will find many artistic items that may well be within your budget.

Before laying the table, bring everything you need into the dining room. I find that collecting together all the items for the layout is helpful in creating designs for the table.

Tables for lunch and dinner parties can be arranged in similar ways, but I prefer to use less decoration or arrangements for lunch parties. For dinner parties I like more elaborate arrangements using darker tones in the table linen. You can be as daring as you like in your combinations as this adds excitement and interest.

Whether you should have a sit-down or a buffet dinner depends on the number of guests you are expecting, and the size of your table. I prefer buffet parties — you can expand your guest list, and it leaves more room on the table to develop your decorative theme. Placing your table in a corner is not always advisable as it can cause crowding. If you have decorative pieces that are not part of the meal, place them in such a way so as not to hinder guests when they serve themselves.

Whether you should use a tablecloth or mats depends on the surface of your dining table. If you have a polished wood table, using only mats can show it off to advantage. Otherwise a table-cloth may be more suitable, and in some cases may look more elegant. Candles are very attractive and can give an atmospheric touch, either placed in candle sticks or in fruits and vegetables as demonstrated in the book.

Attention to detail is important. Make sure that all your cutlery and crockery are clean and sparkling. It is difficult to give an indication of how much time you need to arrange a good table, but once you have tried some of the ideas in the book, your own ideas will develop, and you will pick up speed with experience.

Arrange the plates, cutlery, glasses etc on a side table — this will give you more room on the main table, and makes it easier for guests to help themselves.

Note: You can mix and match the menus in the book with different table layouts.

If you make more food items than the number of serving bowls demonstrated in the book, add more, ensuring that they co-ordinate with the rest of the table.

I have left the serving bowls in my picture empty to demonstrate how you should set out your table before serving the food.

Occasion:
    Wedding or Festive Party

Colour scheme:
    Blue and green

Main dish:
    Peacock Sweet (outer piece)

Vegetable sculpture:
    Blue turnip rose and White Pumpkin candle, 1 large turnip, hosta leaves, 1 medium-sized pumpkin

Accessories:
    Co-ordinating table-cloth, serving bowls and serving spoons, Blue, green and peacock napkins, napkin rings, Peacock feathers

MENU:
    Peacock sweet
    Dhansak (Parsi curry)
    Brown Rice
    Puri
    Kofta curry
    Mung Dal Dhokla
    Corn Gughra
    Spiced Yoghurt (Raita)
    Pickles, Poppadam, Chutney

INGREDIENTS:
FOR DECORATING THE SWEET
    Cashew Nut Barfi
    200 gm. desiccated coconut
    Small carton double cream (142 gm.)
    150 gm. icing sugar
    Blue and green food colour
    1 oblong-shaped black sweet (for the eye)

PEACOCK TABLE *(Photograph on page 17)*

The focal point of this table is the Peacock Sweet. The two vegetable sculptures, the blue rose and the pumpkin candle are placed vertically above the sweet. The rest of the table is arranged around this vertical thread. Having placed the peacock at the end of the table in the centre, arrange the hosta leaves above it in a triangle and place the serving dishes, as displayed in the photograph, with the turnip rose in the centre. Place the pumpkin candle at the top of the triangle. Arrange the napkins in a circle around the centre. Place the peacock feathers inside the napkin rings. For details on how to fold the napkins see page 112 and for instructions on preparing the turnip and pumpkin candle see page 138.

Creating the Peacock Sweet
Prepare the coconut: Mix the dessicated coconut, icing sugar and cream, heat in a thick saucepan until the mixture is non-sticky.

(See recipe for Peacock Sweet [Cashew nut Barfi] on page 45.) Divide the prepared coconut in half. Take a quarter of the coconut and colour it green, and the other quarter blue. Spread the cashew nut barfi evenly onto the board (size 15" by 15"), about 2 cm. thick. Trace a peacock shape onto tracing paper (a tracing has been included.) Place the traced shape onto the board on top of the sweet. Using a sharpened toothpick, pierce holes in it according to the design. Remove the paper and cut out all the peacock part of the sweet, including the legs. Take the blue coconut and spread it neatly across the top half of the peacock's body then take the green coconut and spread it across the bottom half. Cut out small oval shapes around the circle of the peacock, and again a smaller semicircle inside the outer circle. Cut out three ovals directly above the head. Fill these alternately with the green and blue coconut. Fill out the background with the chocolate spread using a brush. Complete the decoration with white sweets and hundreds and thousands, as in the photograph. Finally place the eye and decorate the beak.

Cake Board 15" diameter.
1 oblong-shaped red sweet (for the beak)
30-40 long white sweets for decoration
1 240 gm. box of chocolate spread
Silver & gold "hundreds and thousands"

Occasion:
Wedding Party or Birthday Party

Colour scheme:
Red and white

Main dish:
White Cake (Pistachio and Almond Cake)

Vegetable sculpture:
White radish and tomato basket

Accessories:
White serving dishes, red napkins, flower basket for arranging vegetable sculpture, white radish roses, (see appendix), mixed lettuce leaves, cherry tomatoes

MENU:
Pistachio and Almond Cake (White Cake)
Mango Kadhi
Amiri Pulao
Green Granary Kofta
Puri
Corn Cutlets
Baked Dish
Jacket Potato Curry
Poppadam, pickles

RED AND WHITE TABLE

Arrange the table mats as displayed. Place the flower basket and the white cake on either end of the table. Arrange the serving bowls, and the napkins. Arrange two serving bowls just below the pickle tray, placing large tomato flowers in each.

Making the flower basket:
Make the radish roses using radishes of assorted sizes. Arrange lettuce/salad leaves thickly on the base of the basket, using a pin holder to hold in place. Arrange the radish roses on the salad leaves and the cherry tomatoes inside the radishes. If the radish rose is large enough, cut the tomato roses and place in the centre.

Decorating the cake:
Make the White Cake, the Pista Sweet and the paste (recipe on page 48). Take a round board (30 cm. diameter) and place a well-greased round cake ring 9½" x 2" on it. Spread the almond sweet in the ring, pressing it down firmly with the base of a flat spoon. Spread the pistachio sweet on top of it and press down. Take three-quarters of the paste and roll it out on a sheet of polythene, to the size of the cake ring. Take the remainder of the paste and roll it out in a long horizontal shape, the width of the cake ring and approximately 30 cm. long. Take the first section of the paste and place it on top of the cake. Lift out the cake ring, leaving the cake shape alone. Spread the horizontal strip along the width of the cake, completely covering it. Cover with foil and place in the refrigerator for a day. When ready to use the sweet, remove from the fridge an hour before required. Decorate using an icing sugar bouquet and sugar strawberries.

Note: When the cake is cut, it forms an attractive green and white slice.

Occasion:
Wedding Party, or when the bridegroom (and family) have been invited to the bride's house

Colour scheme:
Green, red and yellow

Main dish:
Bandhani Sweet (almond cake)

No vegetable sculpture, but decorate with fresh flowers.

MENU:
Bandhani Sweet (Almond Cake)
Dal (Lentil Soup)
Tomato Rice
Green Stuffed Vegetable Curry
Puri
Potato Rolls with Kand
Peanut Patties with Corn
Ragda
Raita, pickles, chutney, poppadams

BANDHANI TABLE

Place a red table-cloth on the table and place the sweet in the centre. Arrange the serving plates on serving mats in a semicircle around the centre-piece. Then arrange the three decorative mats with flowers and Indian candles (divas) as shown. Finally fold the napkins (see appendix), place in napkin holder and arrange as shown. Place some additional serving spoons on both horizontal ends of the arrangements.

Decorating/making the Bandhani Sweet:
Make the Almond Cake (recipe on page 52). Roll out the cake on a pastry board (45 cm. x 60 cm.) about 1.5 cm. thick. Trim the edges and put the left over sweet aside. Divide the remainder of the sweet into two equal portions and colour them red and green respectively (using food colour). Trace out a Bandhani (tracing included) design on to tracing paper. Place the paper on the sweet (on board) and pierce out the holes of the design using a tooth-pick. Mix some red and some green food colour in water, and using a very fine paintbrush, paint through the pierced holes. Remove the paper for the main borders i.e. the checks. Take the red sweet prepared previously and roll out on to a pastry board. Cut out small oval shapes. Do the same with the green sweet. Use these shapes to make the borders. Touch up remaining gaps with the food colour paint.

Occasion:
Lunch/Dinner Buffet Party

Colour scheme:
Orange and green

Main dish:
Daffodil Sweet

Vegetable sculpture:
Capsicum and pickle tree

Accessories:
Table-cloth in beige and white, green hosta leaves or leaf-shaped mats, spoons, serving bowls, orange and green napkins, wooden tree-shaped piece.

DAFFODIL TABLE

Fold the green and orange napkins (see appendix). Place the sweet slightly off-centre and place the mats around the sweet. Place the pickle tree on the opposite edge of the table (see picture). Arrange the napkins around the pickle tree. Place the serving bowls on the green mats. Place serving spoons inside the napkins. Arrange dahlias or any other orange flowers as decoration. Tip: instead of pickle tree, cut out 'capsicum bowls' and arrange on a tray.

Decorating the sweet:
Make the 'Daffodil Sweet' and 'Daffodil Sticks' (recipe on page 55). Spread the Daffodil Sweet (carrot halwa) on a board 46 cm. in diameter. Spread some ghee on to a rolling pin and roll out the halwa evenly. Cut out a circle 46 cm. in diameter using the tracing paper. Draw a daffodil on the paper, and cut out. Cut out daffodil and stalk shapes. Place the 'white flower' on to the daffodil shapes, and the 'Daffodil Stick' mixture on to the stalk shapes. Lift out the tracing paper gently. Mix a little yellow food colour in water, then

MENU:
Daffodil Sweet
Corn Curry
Badshahi Vegetables
Chutney Rice
Patra with gravy
Mung and Channa Dal Dhokla
Chopda
Pappad, pickles, chutney, salad.

using a paintbrush, shade the flowers yellow. Similarly, mix a little green food colour in water and shade the leaves green (i.e. the leaves made out of pumpkin halwa as in recipe).

Occasion:
Evening Buffet Party

Colour scheme:
Orange and brown

Main dish:
Mungdal Sweet Doll

Vegetable sculpture:
Carrot and orange flower basket

Accessories:
Brown table-cloth (or pink and brown), co-ordinating mats, pickle-relish bowls, orange, light orange and brown paper napkins, orange candles.

MENU:
Mung Dal Sweet Doll
Navratna Kadhi
Coconut Rice
Naan
Moghlai Potato Curry
Corn Rolls
Damli Dhokra
Pappad, pickles, chutney, salad.

INGREDIENTS: FOR BASKET
Medium sized basket
15-20 small carrots
4-5 small oranges, or kumquats
Sprig of parsley
1 large oasis
Medium sized flat bowl or pan
Toothpicks

SUNSET TABLE

Arrange the table-cloth, placing the flower basket on the top right of the table. Place the Mung Dal Doll in the centre of the table. Arrange the napkins around the doll, and place spoons as shown. The serving dishes can be placed around the outer edges of the table.

Making the carrot and orange basket:
Cut the carrots into flower shapes (see appendix). Place the carrot flowers and parsley in a bowl of water and refrigerate for a few hours. Place a bowl upside down in the basket. Place the oasis on top of this (to give the arrangement height). Arrange the parsley on the oasis, covering it completely to look like a flower bed. Arrange the carrot flowers. Place the oranges inside the carrots, keeping them in place with toothpicks.

Decorating the doll:
Prepare the Mung Dal Sweet (see recipe on page 62). Roll out the marzipan on a pastry board. Grease the jelly mould and line the sides with marzipan, leaving the centre hollow. Press the marzipan into the shape of the mould. Fill in the hollow of the mould with the Mung Dal Sweet. Refrigerate for at least 2 hours then place upside down on a cake board. Wrap a hot towel around the jelly mould for a few seconds to help the sweet slide out neatly. Place the doll's head on top of it. Decorate with sugar flowers. Cover the base of the cake board with the desiccated coconut.

INGREDIENTS: THE DOLL

2 packets of marzipan
1 jelly mould (18 cms diameter,
9 cms depth)
A doll's head
yellow desiccated coconut
(using food colour)
some sugar flowers
one round cake board (30cms
diameter)

Occasion:
Evening Buffet Party

Colour scheme:
Green and white

Main dish:
Daisy Sweet

Vegetable sculpture:
Pickled chillies with celery and
carrot leaves.

Accessories:
Black table-cloth, daisy shaped
serving bowls, green mats,
green and white napkins,
serving spoons.

MENU:

Daisy Sweet
Brinjal Toovar Beans Pulao
Kadhi
Stuffed Tooriya Curry
Punjabi Potato Curry
Masala Naan
Patra Samosas
Pickles, pappad, chutney,
salad.

INGREDIENTS:

FOR THE PICKLED CHILLIES

Leaves from the top of carrots
1 celery stick
Toothpicks
Stuffed chillies
Pin holder

INGREDIENTS:

FOR DECORATING THE SWEET

2 small packets of marzipan
Green food colour

DAISY TABLE

Arrange the sweet and the vegetable pickles on either side of the table. Put the napkins into the napkin rings and arrange in a semicircle between the two pieces. Then arrange the serving bowls in the shape of a daisy, as in the picture.

Decorating the pickled chillies:
Place the celery stick on the pin holder, after separating the leaves. Arrange the carrot leaves around the celery. Place the chillies on the celery tips using toothpicks to keep in place. Stuff chillies with pickle masala or as required.

Decorating the sweet:
Make the sweet (page 64) using a non-stick cake mould/jelly mould approximately 8 cm. in diameter at the bottom, and 16 cm. in diameter at the top. Take the sweet and invert it on to the serving plate. Remove the mould gently by wrapping a hot towel around it. Roll out each packet of marzipan. Colour one portion dark green, and the other light green. Take the light green rolled out marzipan and carefully cut out 10 leaf shapes. Arrange them on the sweet, folded inwards. Repeat using the dark green marzipan, but fold the leaves outwards (as shown).

Occasion:
Birthday Party or Evening Buffet

Colour scheme:
Brown and shocking pink

Main dish:
Royal Cake

Accessories:
Table-cloth, brown and pink mats, serving bowls, candle, pickle bowls, pink flower arrangements, pink napkins, napkin rings, serving spoons.

MENU:
Royal Cake
Panchkuti Dal
Plain Boiled Rice
Kulcha
Khasta Kachori
Undhayu (Surati)
Puffed Rice Dhoklas
Pappad, pickles, chutney, raita.

ROYAL TABLE

Place the prepared sweet (recipe on page 67) at one end of the table, with the pink flower arrangement diagonally opposite at the other end of the table. Place serving mats along the diagonal. Arrange pickle dishes and a candle on either side of the mats. Arrange napkins around the cake. Napkin rings in the shape of roses may be used in this arrangement.

Occasion:
An Evening Buffet Party

Colour scheme:
Brown and gold

Main dish:
Mango Cake

Vegetable sculpture:
Golden Pickle Tree

Accessories:
Brown table-cloth, mats, golden candles, serving spoons and serving plates, brown and gold napkins (the gold ones can be plain or with white dots), cane mats.

BROWN AND GOLD TABLE

Place the cake in the centre of the table as shown. Arrange a bowl of napkins (to look like a flower bowl) e.g. Rainbow fan napkins on one end of the table, and the chilli tree on the other. Arrange serving mats and bowls around this. Use gold candles for a softer look, if required.

Making the chilli tree: (Golden Pickle Tree)
Slit the chillies in the centre and place them in a bowl of water. Refrigerate for a few hours to make them puff out a little. Cut some of them into flower shapes (see appendix). Arrange the branch on to the pin holder on top of a decorative mat. Place the remaining twigs around this, then arrange the chillies by placing through the twigs as shown. Decorate with parsley. To make the piece edible, use small multicoloured capsicums or just yellow capsicums, celery and parsley. Sprinkle with salt and pepper.

MENU:
Mango Cake
Bhatia Kadhi
Mixed Vegetable Curry or
Potato Curry with Green
Chutney
Plain Boiled Rice
Corn Patties
Stuffed Parathas
Salad, pickles, pappad, chutney.

INGREDIENTS:
FOR GOLDEN PICKLE TREE
A thickish twig or thin branch
of a tree
Bunch of parsley
1/4 kg. orange or yellow chillies
Some small twigs or branches
Pin holder

Occasion:
Evening Buffet Party

Colour scheme:
Green and red

Main dish:
Potato Cake

Vegetable sculpture:
Anthurium Flower Vase

Accessories:
Table-cloth, serving mats,
serving bowls and spoons, red
and green napkins, napkin
rings.

MENU:
Potato Cake
Pakoda Kadhi
Biryani
Mava Ghaari (sweet)
Cauliflower Curry
Paneer Curry
Mung Dal Parathas
Pappad, chutney, pickles,
salad.

ANTHURIUM TABLE

Arrange the vegetable sculpture and the potato cake on either end of the table. Arrange the napkins in a semi-straight line between the two pieces. Arrange serving dishes, on mats, in the centre of the table.

Making the 'Anthurium' flower vase:
Place the vase on the board. Put the pin holder in the base of the vase, and place the celery stick in it. Cut the capsicums into heart shapes (two out of each capsicum) using toothpicks. Place a red chilli in the centre of each heart shape. Now arrange these flowers into the stalks of the celery (as shown). Use some leek leaves to hold the capsicum flowers at the bottom of the arrangement. Arrange the remaining leek and salad leaves around the base of the vase.

Decorating the potato cake:
Make the flowers from the chillies by splitting them in the centre, as in photograph, then force the separated parts gently back to form flower shapes. Cut the cabbage into small leaf shapes. Arrange the salad leaves at the bottom of the cake. Place a chilli flower on top (centre) of the cake. Arrange the cabbage leaves around it. Arrange the remainder of the chilli flowers around the cake.

INGREDIENTS:
FOR ANTHURIUM FLOWER
VASE
    A 'ring' flower vase
    3 large red capsicums
    8-9 long red chillies
    Bunch of celery with leaves
    Several salad leaves
    2-3 leek leaves
    Pin holder
    Toothpicks
    Board to place vase on.

INGREDIENTS:
FOR DECORATING THE POTATO
CAKE
    Potato cake (recipe on page 74)
    Several salad leaves
    7-8 small red chillies
    Cabbage leaf

Occasion:
    Silver Anniversary Party

Colour scheme:
    Silver and white

Main dish:
    Anniversary Cake

Accessories:
    White and contrasting
    table-cloth, mats, grey
    napkins, silver bowls and
    spoons, pickle dish, white
    flower arrangement with
    silver candle.

MENU
    Anniversary Cake (white
    pumpkin and carrot cake)
    Kadhi
    Stuffed Rice
    Parathas
    Valor Kofta Curry (Green
    Curry)
    Potato Curry in Corn Sauce
    Kund Patties
    Pappad, chutney, pickles,
    salad.

SILVER ANNIVERSARY TABLE

Make a flower arrangement using white roses or white carnations (or a vegetable arrangement using white radish roses). Place this at the top of the table with the cake directly in front of it. Arrange serving bowls on mats, and napkins around the mats.

Decorating the cake:
Make the cake as in recipe (page 78) Roll out the marzipan. Remove the cake ring and cover completely with white marzipan, spread evenly to make a smooth outer case for the cake. Decorate with the flower bouquet and silver leaves. Use a silver board or silver doily to place the cake on. (13" x 13" square)

INGREDIENTS:
FOR DECORATING THE CAKE
    2 packets marzipan
    High flower bouquet
    Some silver leaves

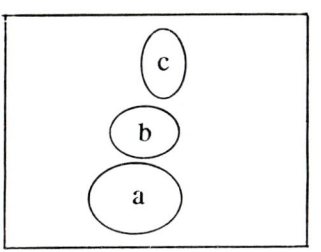

THE PEACOCK TABLE
with pumpkin candle
and turnip rose.

a-Peacock sweet
b-Turnip rose
c-White pumpkin candle

a-White cake
b-White radish and
tomato basket

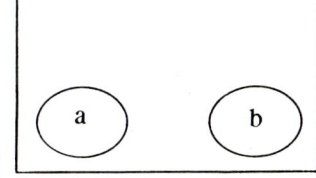

RED AND WHITE TABLE

BANDHANI TABLE
with Bandhani sweet
(centrepiece)

a-Daffodil sweet
b-Capsicum and
pickle tree

DAFFODIL TABLE

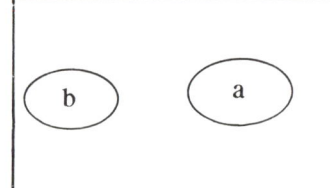

SUNSET TABLE
with moongdal sweet doll
and carrot and orange basket

MOONGDAL SWEET DOLL

**CARROT AND ORANGE
BASKET**

19

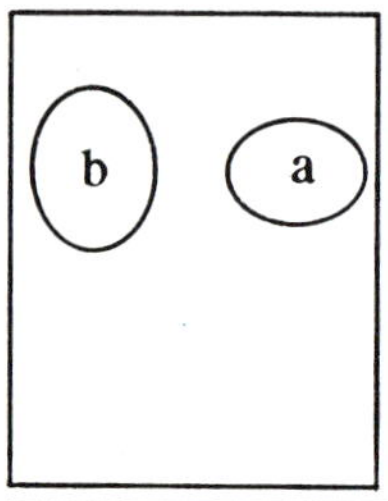

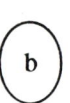

DAISY TABLE

a-Daisy sweet
b-Pickled chillies

ROYAL TABLE

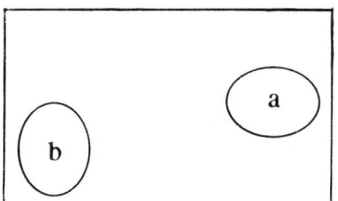

a-Pink flower arrangement
b-Royal cake

ROYAL CAKE

BROWN AND GOLD TABLE
with mango cake and
golden pickle tree

MANGO CAKE

22

ANTHURIUM FLOWER VASE

POTATO CAKE

ANTHURIUM TABLE
with potato cake and
anthurium flower vase

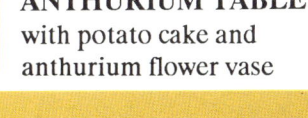

SILVER ANNIVERSARY TABLE
with anniversary cake

a- Onion flower basket
b-Sweet flower cake

CRYSTAL TABLE

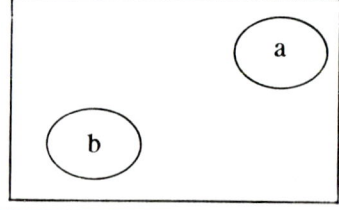

Occasion:
    Evening Buffet Party

Colour scheme:
    Light blue, dark blue and crystal

Main dish:
    Sweet Flower Basket

Vegetable sculpture:
    Onion Flower Basket

Accessories:
    Table-cloth, mats, crystal or glass serving bowls, serving spoons, napkin rings and napkins in two shades of blue, blue candle with blue flower napkin ring.

MENU
    Sweet Flower Basket
    Moghlai Dal
    Three-in-one Rice
    Coriander Paratha
    Potato in Coconut Milk
    Mange-tout and Kofta Curry
    Capsicum Bhajias
    Pappad, pickles, raita, salad.

INGREDIENTS:
FOR SWEET FLOWER BASKET
    Half a packet of marzipan
    Red, blue and green food colours

INGREDIENTS:
FOR ONION FLOWER BASKET
    1 leek
    1 stick of celery
    1 bunch long spring onions
    some oblong shaped onions
    ¼ kg. black grapes
    Round basket
    Oblong basket
    Pin holder
    Toothpicks

CRYSTAL TABLE

Place the sweet basket and the onion basket diagonally opposite each other. Arrange serving bowls in a line through the centre. Arrange napkins around the serving bowls.

Decorating the sweet:
Make the Sweet Flower Cake (page 81) (coconut and marva). Take half the marzipan and colour it green. Take out the other half and colour half of that red, and the rest blue. Cut out red flower shapes from the marzipan and arrange over the sweet as shown. Cut out long green leaf shapes and arrange over the sweet. Make small balls out of the blue marzipan and place in the centre of the flowers.

Making the onion flower basket:
Place the baskets on top of each other as shown. Arrange the leek at the base of the round basket. Place pin holder at the base and arrange the celery stick upright in the pin holder. Separate out the celery stalks as shown. Arrange the spring onions around the rest of the arrangement. Make some onion flowers (see appendix) and refrigerate in cold water with a little blue food colour for at least three hours. Place the onion flowers on the celery and onion stalks securing with toothpicks.

Occasion:
Luncheon Buffet

Colour scheme:
Pink and maroon

Main dish:
Milk Ghaari

Vegetable sculpture:
Rhubarb and radish arrangement (Moon Vase)

Accessories:
Table-cloth, mats, serving bowls, glasses, pink and maroon napkins, vegetable flowers

MENU
Milk Ghaari
Chana Bhatura
Spanish Rice
Green peas, Potato and Mange-tout Curry
Dahi Ghughra
Potato and Nut Curry
Pappad, pickles, chutney, salad.

INGREDIENTS:
FOR VEGETABLE SCULPTURE
Ring-shaped vase
4-5 rhubarb sticks
10-15 radish roses (or cherry tomatoes)

INGREDIENTS:
FOR DECORATING THE SWEET
10 - 12 almonds
Some red and green food colours

MOON TABLE

Arrange the sweet in the centre of the table with the radish basket directly behind it. Arrange the serving bowls, plates and glasses on either side. Place napkins in the glasses as shown.

Making the Moon vase:
Take each rhubarb stick and splice it, making 3-4 cuts from the top, following it through until six inches from the bottom of the stick. Place in cold water and freeze for a few hours to take shape. Make the radish flowers (see appendix). Take the moon-shaped vase and place a pin holder in the base. Place the ends of the rhubarb sticks on the pin holder. Arrange the radish flowers on the rhubarb branches using toothpicks to secure them in place.

Decorating the sweet:
Make the sweet (page 84) and shape into patties, leaving some aside. Take the left-over sweet and mix a little green food colour in it. Take 10-12 almonds and place in boiling water for approximately 3 minutes. Remove from heat and peel off the skin. Colour, using red food colour, and slice into petal shapes. Decorate the sweet using almond petals and green Ghaari to make flowers and stalks.

Occasion:
Luncheon Buffet Party

Colour scheme:
Maroon and violet

Main dish:
Date Sweet (Khajur Ghaari)

Vegetable sculpture:
Aubergine and onion vase

Accessories:
Maroon table mats, maroon
and violet 'boat-shaped'
napkins, serving plates,
spoons, glasses, maroon and
violet candle-sticks and
candle holder.

MENU
Khajur Ghaari (Date Sweet)
Shahi Dal
Rice
Parathas
Rava Corn Dhoklas
Corn Rolls
Haricot Beans in Coconut
Milk (Green Toovar)
Cream Ball Curry
Raita, pappad, pickles, chutney

INGREDIENTS:
FOR AUBERGINE AND ONION
VASE
1 large, slightly unripe aubergine
Chinese leaf or similar salad
leaves
1 large onion
Several small onions
Red cabbage leaves
Toothpicks

MAROON VIOLET TABLE

Arrange the table mats as shown. Place the aubergine vase and the sweet dish horizontally on the top half of the table and arrange the glasses in circles around these two pieces with the napkins between the glasses. Arrange the remaining serving bowls and spoons, as shown.

Making the vegetable sculpture:
Cut the small onion into roses (see appendix). Place in bowl of pink or red food colour and refrigerate for at least an hour. Repeat using the large onion, but allow the petals to separate as shown. Arrange the salad leaves on a circular (slightly hollow, if possible) plate. Place the aubergine on the top half of the plate with the large onion flower in front of it. Cut out the red cabbage leaves into large petal shapes, and arrange them around the top of the aubergine using toothpicks to hold them in place. Arrange the onion roses on these leaves. Arrange the remaining onion roses around the base of the arrangement.

Occasion:
Festival — Lunch or Dinner Buffet Table

Colour scheme:
Orange and green

Main dish:
Sunflower Sweet

Vegetable sculpture:
Cucumber boat

Accessories:
Yellow onion basket, capsicum pickle bowls, sunflower mats, yellow and green napkins

MENU
Sunflower Sweet
Sindhi Kadhi
Chopda
Bread Ghughra
French Bean Curry
Royal Dam Aloo
Corn Rice
Chutney, pappad, pickles, salad

INGREDIENTS:
FOR THE SWEET DECORATION
1/4 kg. coconut powder
Green food colour
Round chocolates e.g. Maltesers
A Chocolate butterfly
A large cake board (13" diam.)

INGREDIENTS:
FOR CUCUMBER BOAT
1 long yellow cucumber (or pumpkin)
1 medium-sized carrot
Parsley, mint or coriander leaves

INGREDIENTS:
FOR ONION BASKET
4-5 large green hostas leaves
7-8 green chillies
1 large onion
1 small basket

SUNFLOWER TABLE

Place the prepared Sunflower Sweet at the centre of the table. Arrange the napkins in a semicircle behind it. Place the capsicum pickle bowls and the onion basket on either side of the sweet (using the mats as bases). Place the cucumber boat in front, as shown.

Decorating the sweet:
Make the sweet. (Recipe on page 90). Arrange the sweet in a circle on the serving plate. Cut out triangled edges as shown. Fill the edges of the sweet with the green desiccated coconut. Decorate the centre of the sweet with chocolate balls. Top with the chocolate butterfly.

Making the cucumber boat:
Hollow out one half of the cucumber, leaving a bridge in the centre. Using a knife, serrate the edges to give it a spiky effect. Arrange this boat on a bed of parsley or mint or coriander leaves. Slice the carrot lengthways into a thin long flat strip. Shape, using a knife, into the shape of a man (you can use man-shaped biscuit moulds as a guide). Place these on each half of the cucumber boat.

Making the onion basket:
Cut the onion into a flower shape, soak in yellow food-coloured water and refrigerate for two hours. Arrange the leaves at the base of the basket. Place the onion flower in the centre of it, and arrange the chillies around the onion.

For the pickle bowls:
4 large capsicums (2 yellow, 2 green)
Cut out the tops and remove the flesh. Place the pickles inside the capsicums and cover with the capsicum lids.

Occasion:
Any time during the Diwali Festival (Indian Christmas)

Colour scheme:
Red and cream

Main dish:
Sweet assortment

Vegetable sculpture:
Flower Rangoli with candles (divas)

Accessories:
Silver serving dishes and spoons, red and white mats, red and white napkins, clay diva stands (or small candle stands), fresh or artificial flowers.

INGREDIENTS:
FOR FLOWER RANGOLI
An assortment of small fresh or artificial flowers
Paisley or mango shaped board
Oasis of roughly the same size
7-8 clay divas
1 large brass diva
Several green leaves

DIWALI TABLE

Arrange the sweet assortment in a flower shape at one end of the table. Place the flower Rangoli at the other end of the table. Arrange a mat, with spoons on a spoon rest, at the centre of these two pieces. Arrange serving bowls and napkins around the rest of the table as shown.

Making the Rangoli:
Cut out the oasis in the shape of the board and place it on the board using green adhesive tape (the kind used in floristry). Arrange the flowers densely all over the board, placing the red ones around the centre of the larger end of the board. Place the brass diva in the middle of the red flower circle. Arrange the rest of the divas around the board on three leaves each, as shown. Light the divas just before the guests arrive. For making and decorating the sweets see recipes on page 98. Any of the more formal menus described earlier can be used in this table arrangement.

Occasion:
Cocktail Party

Colour scheme:
Cream and white

Accessories:
Co-ordinating cocktail napkins, cocktail sticks, white lace table-cloth

INGREDIENTS:
Long French bread stick (approximately 60 cm. long)
1 large unsliced loaf of brown bread

TRAIN TABLE

This table has as its centrepiece a bread train with cocktail glasses and canapés arranged around it. Arrange the train on the top half of the table. Arrange some of the cocktail glasses at the base of the train with long cherry-topped cocktail sticks.

How to make the train:
Arrange the train on a large piece of silver foil.
Take the long French bread and cut out a quarter of it. Cut out a small slice and keep aside. Take the remaining piece and divide into 4 equal portions by hollowing out the bread, approximately 5 cm. deep i.e. take the first quarter of the remaining piece and hollow out. Then leave some unhollowed bread of say, 1.5 cm., and repeat the process with the next quarter, and so on. The finished piece should have four hollows of approximately 10 cm. in length,

29

1 small packet of cocktail
bread snacks (wheel shaped)
12 crostini or bread sticks
(approximately 30 cm. long)
1/4 kg. of medium-hard Cheddar cheese
1 tin of cherries or 1/4 kg. of
fresh cherries
1 small pineapple or tin equivalent
2-3 packets of Hula Hoops
1/4 kg. of roasted salted peanuts
125 gm. green leaves
Toothpicks
Round Ritz cheese crackers (8
or 10)
Silver foil

and approximately 5 cm. in depth, with bread 'bridges' in between of approximately 2.5 cm. in length. This should resemble carriages. Hollow out the main large loaf of bread to resemble a tunnel as shown. Place the tunnel at the top. Arrange the crostini vertically, as shown, to resemble rails. Chop the remaining bread sticks or crostini into smaller 5-8 cm. pieces and arrange them horizontally to resemble tracks. Now place the rest of the first quarter of the French bread as shown. Leave a gap and arrange the rest of the prepared French bread. Connect the two pieces i.e. the gap, using a wheel-shaped bread snack and a toothpick. Take the small slice of bread cut out earlier and arrange it neatly on top of the first quarter on the French bread to resemble an engine. Pipe with cream cheese to complete the effect of the engine. You can substitute with Cheddar cheese to achieve more or less the same effect. Arrange the wheels as shown, using Ritz crackers and toothpicks. If the biscuits are too crumbly, try leaning them against the bread without the support of the toothpicks. If that does not work, cut out wheels using the Cheddar cheese and use that instead, securing with toothpicks. Prepare cocktail nibbles, using toothpicks or cocktail sticks and arranging the cheese, olives, bread, cherries and Hula Hoops as shown. You can mix and match these as required. Arrange the cocktail sticks in the four hollows i.e. carriages, and on top of the tunnel as shown. Decorate the rest of the train with peanuts, biscuits, etc.

Note: The glasses have been 'frosted'. To do this place some lemon juice in a saucer, and some sugar in another. Dip the rim of each glass first in the lemon juice and then in the sugar, to form a thin coating. Place in the refrigerator for at least one hour.

INGREDIENTS:

TO MAKE THE RHUBARB
TREE
   A Base for the arrangement
5-6 long rhubarb sticks
Salad leaves
Prepared cocktail snacks on
toothpicks or cocktail sticks
3-4 large pin holders

THE RHUBARB TREE:

This is also a cocktail party table with the rhubarb tree as the centrepiece. Glasses and canapés can be arranged around it.

How to make the rhubarb tree:
Take each rhubarb stick and slice it lengthways from the top to about 8-10 cm. from the base. Refrigerate in ice cold water for at least 2-3 hours. Arrange on to a pin holder, and gently pull back the separated sections of the sticks. Arrange the cocktail snacks on the white portion of the rhubarb sticks using toothpicks. Decorate with salad leaves and the remaining cocktail snacks. Cocktail snacks contain: bread, cheese, pineapple, cherries, olives, etc.

Occasion:
Cocktail Party
(Although used as a cocktail party table here, this can be adapted and used for informal lunches, dinners, etc.)

Colour scheme:
Green, burgundy, yellow and orange

Accessories:
Yellow and burgundy napkins, green leaves, serving spoons, etc., 15-20 asparagus sticks, melon bowls.

SAMPLE MENU
(if using as a lunch table):
Recipes nos. 28-34
Pineapple Sweet (as in picture)
Mung Dal
Plain Rice
Parathas
Mixed Dal Dhoklas
Paneer Pea Curry
Corn Chops
Aubergines in Gravy
Pappad, pickles and raita

INGREDIENTS:
FOR MAKING MELON
BOWLS
1 long melon
3-4 ball-shaped melons or white pumpkins

MELON TABLE

Place the sweet at the top of the table. Arrange the asparagus to resemble the branches of a tree. Place leaves and mats at the top of each branch and arrange serving bowls on the mats. Use the main melon bowl, protected by clingfilm, for one of the dishes. Some of the melon bowls can be used for pickles.

Decorating the sweet:
Prepare the sweet as in the recipe. Arrange it in an 'S' shape on a board (12" diameter) and decorate as shown with coloured almonds. (Cut almonds in thin leaf-like shapes and colour using red and green food colour.) Arrange cherries around it. Spread yellow desiccated coconut as a background.
When using the table for a cocktail party:
There will not be a sweet, so arrange cocktail glasses at the top of the table. Arrange canapés or cocktail snacks in the melon bowls (protected by clingfilm). Arrange the remaining melon bowls, and place the napkins down the centre of the table. Use two/three fan shaped napkins and fasten using napkin ring.

How to make the melon bowls:
Divide two of the melons into halves. Serrate the edges using a knife, and arrange in a diagonal. Cut out the tops of the remaining two melons (about quarter of the way down). Serrate the edges and arrange these in a diagonal. Cut the long melon in half and serrate the edges. Scoop out all the flesh before using as serving bowls.

Note: You can substitute ordinary serving bowls for melon bowls when using the table for a dinner party setting.

Occasion:
Children's Party

Colour scheme:
Green, yellow and red

Main dish:
Party sweet in the shape of a house.

Accessories:
Napkins, napkin rings, serving dishes, pineapple, flower arrangement, etc.

INGREDIENTS:
FOR SWEET HOUSE
4 250 gm. packets of marzipan
4.5 kg. of prepared sweet (any of the sweet recipes in Section Two)
e.g. Carrot Halwa
1/4 kg. desiccated coconut (coloured green using food colour)
Bread sticks or long biscuit sticks
Eggcups and plastic trees for decoration
Marzipan animals and flowers
1 cake mould or box (20 cm. x 15 cm.)
A cake board (13" x 13" square)

INGREDIENTS:
FOR VEGETABLE FLOWER ARRANGEMENT
Conical shaped vase
Small red beetroots
Red chillies
Mint leaves
White radish flower
Cherry or cherry tomato
Sticks of Sargva Sing
Rhubarb Sticks

PINEAPPLE TABLE

This table can also be adapted for use as an informal lunch or supper party table. Arrange the four mats as shown. Place the 'house' in the centre of the table, with the napkins directly in front of it resembling rays. Place the pineapple/flower arrangement on one side of the house, and the serving dishes on the other side. Place a decorated cocktail glass or vase at one end of the top half of the table (diagonally opposite the first pineapple/flower arrangement), and the remaining serving dishes (in this case decorative relish bowls, and pineapples used as relish bowls) at the other end of the table. Finish by arranging the napkins in semicircles around the relish tray and the vase.

How to make the sweet 'house':
Make the sweet and place 3 kg. of the sweet in the cake mould or box. Refrigerate until set. Remove gently and place on a serving plate. Take two packets of the marzipan and colour it orange. Keep aside two tablespoons and roll out the rest thinly. Now gently cover the rectangular sweet with the orange marzipan. Take the remaining 1.5 kg. of the sweet and place it on top of the rectangle, shaping it gently to form a 'roof'. Take the remaining two packets of marzipan and colour this brown. Keep aside 4 tablespoons of the brown marzipan and roll out the rest thinly. Cover the 'roof' with the brown marzipan. Use the remaining orange marzipan to make windows in the 'roof'. Use the remaining brown marzipan to make a door and windows. Use a knife to shape the windows and door, and use contrasting marzipan to make the window panes. Decorate with sugar flowers, arrange the animals and place the eggcups at the front of the house with the little plastic trees in them. Finish with chocolate drops, etc, if required.

Note: Measurements of the box and the exact dimensions of the roof are shown in a diagram in the appendix.

Making the flower vase:
Arrange the Sing sticks in the vase. Using toothpicks arrange the capsicum flowers, and the radish flower. Arrange the mint leaves and red chillies as shown. Complete with cherry tomato in the radish flower and radish pieces arranged in the beetroot flowers.

For the pineapple arrangement: Arrange radish flowers on rhubarb sticks with cherry tomatoes.

MOON TABLE
with milk ghaari
and moon vase

MOON VASE
(rhubarb and radish
arrangement)

MAROON VIOLET TABLE

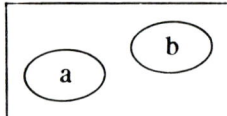

a-Date sweet
b-Aubergine and onion vase

a-Sunflower sweet
b-Cucumber boat

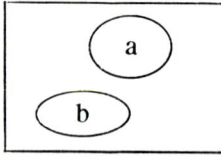

SUNFLOWER TABLE

DIWALI TABLE
with sweet assortment
and flower rangoli

DIWALI SWEET ASSORTMENT

35

THE RHUBARB TREE

TRAIN TABLE

MELON TABLE

MELON BOWLS

VEGETABLE FLOWER ARRANGEMENTS

PINEAPPLE TABLE
with sweet house and
vegetable flower arrangements

TURNIP FLOWER ARRANGEMENT

ROSE TABLE
with turnip flower
arrangement

39

a-Carrot ghaari
b-Strawberry ghugharas
c-Strawberry samosas
d-Sweet turban
e-Sweet sari

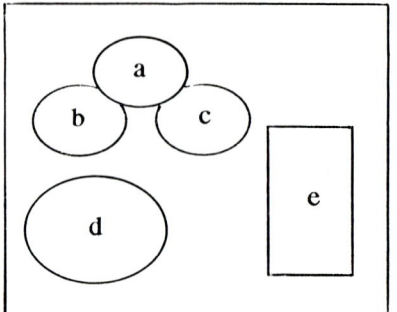

A SELECTION OF INDIAN WEDDING PARTY SWEETS

Occasion:

Casual Supper Party

Colour scheme:

Turquoise and yellow

Accessories:

Turquoise and yellow napkins, turnip rose arrangement, serving plates, spoons, etc., cork mats, napkin rings

Menu:

Can be adapted from any of the earlier tables.

INGREDIENTS:
FOR TURNIP FLOWER ARRANGEMENT

Glass bowl flower vase — available in most department stores. (These separate into three parts which each contain three glass bowls which can be stacked on top of each other at different angles.)
Prepared turnip roses (see appendix)
Yellow food colour
Green and blue food colour

THE ROSE TABLE

Note: This table can be adapted for a different occasion by using silver serving dishes and more elaborate flower arrangements. Fold the napkins as shown (see appendix) and arrange in a mango shape, interspersing with spoons. Place a pickle dish or any other ornamental dish in the centre. Place the radish flower arrangement at the bottom right-hand side of the table, on a cork mat. Arrange serving dishes in a semicircle around it. Arrange serving bowls on top as shown.

How to make turnip flower arrangement:
Colour the turnips yellow by soaking in coloured water for a few hours in the refrigerator. Fill the vase with water coloured turquoise by mixing blue and green food colours. Arrange the turnip roses in the glass bowls using toothpicks to secure the arrangement in place. Any of the menus in this book are suitable for use on this table.

A SAMPLE DISPLAY OF VEGETABLE FLORISTRY AND DECORATIVE FOOD

(See photograph on page 129)

From left to right (clockwise):
1. Onion and radish and turnip flowers arranged round a backdrop of a wooden 'tree'.
2. Turnip flower arrangement in an 'eight' shaped container
3. An Exotic Salad
4. Coconut and Pistachio Sandesh.
5. Blue radish flower vases.

Explanatory notes.

The turnip and onion flowers have been cut as explained in the 'Vegetable Floristry' section. Use large round radishes for maximum effect. Soak the prepared flowers in the appropriate coloured water, and refrigerate for a few hours before use.

1. Onion rings have been placed round the branches of the tree. A few leeks have been placed behind the tree to give a wooded effect. Maroon and green cabbage leaves have been placed on a flattish vase with a large radish flower forming the centrepiece.

2. Again, two large turnip flowers have been arranged as central points in an 'eight shaped' vase, surrounded by red and green cabbage leaves.

3. The salad has been made using a rectangular loaf tin as a mould. The salad has been placed in the centre of a serving plate, decorated with red chillies, capsicums, and turnip flowers.

4. The coconut sandesh (peach and white), and the pistachio sandesh (green and white) can be decorated with marzipan flowers, or icing strands.

5. The two tall black vases have one blue turnip flower each, some cabbage leaves as foliage, and you can use any other items as additional foliage. In the picture I have used 'Ikebana' twigs, and leek leaves.

p.30   Under ingredients (Train Table)
        For 125 gm. green leaves
        Read 125 gm. green olives

p.57   Recipe 25
        Under ingredients
        Add 6-7 cups of water
               Foil to cover
        Under method, after the words: 'pour this hot seasoned water on to the rolled leaves'
        Add Cover with foil.

p.58   Recipe 26
        Under ingredients for the Vaghaar
        Delete 6-7 cups water
               Foil to cover

p.64   Recipe 42
        Under method, after the words: 'Gently mix the ghee with the milk powder'
        Add Make 2 taar syrup with the sugar and water.
        Add chhanno to the syrup and mix thoroughly.

p.68   Recipe 48
        Under method Part 4, in the sentence: 'Take the second portion of the date mixture (Part 1) and place
        this on top of the mava mixture.
        For mava mixture
        Read coconut mixture

p.69   Recipe 51
        Under ingredients
        '1 tsp. cinnamon, cloves, pepper (mixed)'
        Add the word: ground

p.80   Recipe 70
        Under ingredients for stuffing
        Delete Pinch of asafoetida

p.98   Recipe 102
        Under ingredients
        Add $^3/_4$ cup icing sugar

p.120   Under General tips for punches
        For 'sea salt'
        Read 'Black salt'

p.134   Under Turnip Rose
        Add the words (under 1)
        and place upside down (i.e. root on top)

p.136   Under Turnip Flower
        Delete the words (under 1)
        and place upside down (i.e. root on top)

p.139   Under D) mava
        Ingredients should read:
                To make 450 gm. (1 lb. of mava)
                4 pints full cream milk (red top)
                4 tbsp. milk powder

p.139   Under E) Paneer (Chhanno)
        Ingredients should read:
                4 pints of milk (red top)
                $^1/_2$ tsp. citric acid or lemon juice
        Delete the line that reads
                'To make 450 gm. (1 lb.) of mava'

Recipes

An Introduction to Indian Sweets

For many years, or rather centuries, on special occasions such as marriages, the birth of a child, birthdays, etc. Indians have celebrated by preparing a feast in which one or more of the main dishes are sweets.

Our traditional sweets include 'Ladva', 'Siro', 'Jambu', 'Jalebi', 'Mesub' and 'Monthal'. We can divide Indian sweets into four broad categories, according to their ingredients:

1) Gram flour, wheat flour, white flour, rice flour, semolina
2) Mava, i.e. thickened boiled milk
3) 'Chhano', i.e. curdled milk
4) Vegetables and fruits.

While I have included some traditional sweet recipes, I have particulary concentrated on non-traditional sweets and their decoration.

Most traditional sweets are rich in ghee and sugar, and consequently have diminished in popularity, particularly with the health conscious. I have tried, therefore, to include more Indian sweets made using curdled milk as a lighter alternative.

Curdled milk has less cholesterol than ghee (a butter extract used in traditional recipes). It is easier to digest and therefore probably more suitable to urban living. One can also reduce the amount of sugar used, or use sugar substitutes to reduce the calories.

Vegetarians who do not eat eggs can enjoy these sweets, suitably decorated for birthdays and anniversaries.

Decoration

Indian sweets, once they have been prepared are normally spread on a plate and cut into square and diamond shapes, or rolled into a ball. I have tried to decorate both traditional and non-traditional sweets using more exciting shapes and designs, some of which are similar to cakes in Western cooking.

Decorating sweets imaginatively can add a new dimension, and will make them look even more appetizing. I have demonstrated some of my ideas and hope you will enjoy trying them. They are simple and interesting and can bring fun and pride to your work. Once you know the basic steps you can create your own designs. Everyone has their own artistic style, and a little decoration can make a simple dish look like a work of art. I hope this book will give you the basic information to help you develop your own ideas. Practice will help your confidence and ability, and gradually you will build up speed.

It is important to co-ordinate the colour and design of your decoration with the table-cloth and napkins that you intend to use. I have found that using colourful decorations and napkins is an easy way to develop a theme on a table and give it that 'something extra'.

The ingredients I have used for decoration are quite exotic but easy to buy. (Almonds, pistachios, cashew nuts and desiccated coconut for example.) You can also use other items more usually used in decorating cakes, such as icing sugar, chocolate and marzipan.

I generally do not use ready-made food colours, as they are sometimes considered harmful. I make my own food colour from sources such as fruits, vegetables and chocolate powder.

Storage

Normally these sweets keep their freshness for at least one or two weeks. Traditional sweets made from various flours can be kept in air-tight containers for three to four weeks. Sweets made from fruit, vegetables and milk bases should be refrigerated, but should also last three to four weeks.

All these sweets can be kept for a maximum of 3 months if stored in a deep freeze. This is very useful as they can be prepared in advance, allowing 3-4 hours to defrost. They can also be decorated in advance and kept in the refrigerator but they should be removed two hours before serving.

INGREDIENTS:

4 cups (32 oz.) ground cashews
2 cups (16 oz.) grated mava
2 cups (16 oz.) sugar
2 tbsp. ghee
3/4 cup water
1/2 tsp. cardamom powder

1: CASHEW NUT BARFI

Heat the ghee in a medium-sized saucepan and add the cashews. Roast over a low flame for 3 minutes. Add the mava, stir and remove from heat. Heat the water and sugar in a separate pan and make 3 taar syrup. Add the cashew mixture to the syrup. Allow to cool for 10 minutes. Add the Cardamom powder. The sweet is now ready to spread if required.

INGREDIENTS:

3/4 cup (6 oz.) toover dal
1 tbsp. channa dal
1 tbsp. masoor dal
225 gm. (8 oz.) liquidized tomatoes
1 tbsp. ghee
1 tbsp. chopped ginger and chillies
6 cloves garlic
1 tsp. chilli powder
1 tsp. turmeric powder
1 medium-sized potato
115 gm. (4 oz.) white pumpkin
115 gm. (4 oz.) aubergine
1 cup (8 oz.) fenugreek leaves
1 onion
1 tbsp. chopped coriander leaves
Salt, sugar and lemon to taste

Masala for paste:
1 tsp. coriander seeds
1 tsp. cumin seeds
4 sticks cinnamon
4 cloves
4 cardamoms (black or green)
6 peppers
1 tbsp. fennel seeds
2 tbsp. grated coconut
Roast all these ingredients and grind into a powder.

2: DHANSAK (PARSI CURRY)

Wash all the dals under hot running water. Liquidize the tomatoes chopped onions and garlic. Chop all the vegetables. Put 4-5 cups of water in a pressure cooker and put in all the dals and vegetables. Boil the mixture over a low flame for 20 minutes. Allow to cool, and liquidize. Heat the ghee in a saucepan, add the masala paste, chillies, ginger, tomatoes, onion and garlic and fry for 5 minutes. Add the dal/vegetable mixture, salt, chilli powder, turmeric powder, sugar and lemon, and boil for 10 minutes.
Serves 8-10.

INGREDIENTS:

2 cups (16 oz.) basmati rice
(or brown rice, or Uncle Ben's
whitegrain)
2 tbsp. ghee
3 onions
1 tbsp. cumin seeds
Salt to taste
1 tbsp. sugar

3: BROWN RICE

Cook the rice as normal. Heat a saucepan, add ghee and fry the onions. Add cumin seeds and sugar when the mixture is brownish in colour. Add the cooked rice and mix well. One tablespoon of soya sauce added to the mixture will make the rice browner. Serves 8-10.

INGREDIENTS:

1 cup (8 oz.) wholemeal flour
1 tbsp. oil
3-4 cups oil in a deep frying
pan
Water to make dough

4: PURI

Mix the oil in the flour to make a powdery dough. Add water until it forms a consistent texture, kneading thoroughly as the dough must not be soft. Divide into about 18 portions, rolling each portion into a round even circle about 5 cm. in diameter.

Method for frying Puris:
Heat oil in a fryer or deep frying pan. Fry the puris lightly until they puff up and turn them over to fry the other side. Remove from heat, drain, and place on to kitchen paper towels. Serve hot. Serves 4-5.

INGREDIENTS:

450 gm. (1 lb.) green peas
450 gm. (1 lb.) white pumpkin
55 gm. (2 oz.) creamed coconut
450 gm. (1 lb.) liquidized
tomatoes
6 tbsp. chopped ginger and
chillies
1 tbsp. coriander leaves
1 tsp. salt, sugar to taste.

For the paste:
2 onions
1 piece of ginger
6 cloves of garlic
1 tbsp. poppy seeds
4 cloves
4 cinnamon sticks
1 tbsp. coriander and cumin
seeds

For the Kofta:
1 cup (8 oz.) fenugreek leaves
1/2 cup (4 oz.) boiled fresh or
frozen peas
1/2 cup (4 oz.) grated carrot
1/2 cup (4 oz.) boiled, mashed
potatoes

5: KOFTA CURRY

Wash the fenugreek leaves and grind in a liquidizer. Add the peas, carrots, potatoes, beans and all ingredients except the bread. Soak the bread in water, squeeze out, and add to the mixture. Mix thoroughly and divide the mixture into small balls, deep fry and set aside. Boil the peas. Chop the pumpkin finely and boil. Heat the oil in a frying pan and add the paste, tomatoes, creamed coconut, ginger, chillies, chopped coriander, salt, sugar, chilli powder, turmeric powder, peas and pumpkin and boil for 5-7 minutes. Add the koftas (balls) and boil for 2-3 minutes. Serve hot. Serves 8-10.

½ cup (4 oz.) chopped, boiled
beans
4 slices of white bread
Juice of 1 lemon
1 tsp. garam masala
Oil for deep frying
Salt and sugar to taste

INGREDIENTS:

2 cups (16 oz.) green mung dal
(unshelled)
1 tsp. salt
½ tsp. bicarbonate of soda
1 pinch asafoetida
½ cup (4 oz.) natural yoghurt
1 tbsp. chopped ginger and
chillies
1 tbsp. chopped coriander

For the seasoning:
2 tbsp. oil
½ tsp. mustard seeds
½ tsp. cumin seeds
½ tsp. sesame seeds

6: MUNG DAL DHOKLA

Wash the mung dal under running water. Soak overnight or for 6-7 hours. Grind thoroughly in a liquidizer, with yoghurt. Keep the mixture aside for 4-5 hours. Add the salt, ginger, asafoetida, chillies and bicarbonate of soda. Mix thoroughly. Boil some water in a deep vessel or a double boiler. Place a large heatproof (steel) dish in it — a thali if possible. Brush the dish with oil. Place 4 tablespoons of the mixture in the dish and spread evenly. Cover and boil for 10 minutes. Remove from the heat and cut into diamond shapes. Add seasoning and serve hot.

For the seasoning:
Heat the oil and add the seeds and when it starts crackling remove from heat and add to the prepared dhokla (on top).
Variation: Cut the dhoklas into long sticks (the shape of chips), deep fry and serve with drinks.
Serves 8-10.

INGREDIENTS:

1 cup (8 oz.) wholemeal flour
1 tbsp. semolina
½ tsp. salt
1 tbsp. oil
Oil for deep frying

For the stuffing:
225 gm. (8 oz.) boiled or frozen
corn
1 tsp. salt
1 tsp. sugar
Juice 1 lemon
1 tbsp. ground peanuts
1 tsp. cornflour mixed with
dessertspoon water
1 dessertspoon butter or oil
1 dessertspoon ground ginger
and chillies
1 dessertspoon chopped
coriander
1 dessertspoon chopped
cashew nuts

7: CORN GHUGHARA (CORN ROLLS)

Mix the semolina, salt and flour. Pour the oil into the flour mixture, add water gradually, and make a dough. Knead thoroughly and keep aside while making the stuffing. Mix all the ingredients for the stuffing in a saucepan and cook over a low flame for 10 minutes. Remove from heat and allow to cool. Divide the dough into 10-12 portions. Roll out into small circles (as for Puris — Recipe No. 4). Place 2 tsp. of the corn mixture on half of the Puri and cover it with the second half. Press both halves together and trim the edges to make a design. Deep fry and serve hot.
Serves 4-5.

INGREDIENTS:

170 gm. (6 oz.) ground pistachio (for B)
170 gm. (6 oz.) ground almonds (for A)
170 gm. (6 oz.) milk powder
85 gm (3 oz.) sugar
1/2 cup water
75 ml. (2 1/2 fluid ounces) double cream
1/4 tsp. ground cardamom
1/4 tsp. ground nutmeg
1/4 tsp. ground saffron
1 tbsp. ghee
1 red and white icing sugar flower bouquet
1 25 cm. diameter cake ring with opening latch

C) For the paste:

3.6 litres (6 pints) full cream milk (for chhanno)
4 tbsp. milk powder
1 tsp. ghee
1/2 cup (4 oz.) sugar
1/2 cup water

8: WHITE CAKE (PISTACHIO AND ALMOND CAKE)

A) Almond cake:
Heat the ghee and fry the almonds for 2 minutes. Put aside. Boil the sugar in water in a pan and make 'two taar' syrup. Add all the rest of the ingredients and mix well. Remove from heat and allow to cool.

B) Pistachio cake:
As for the above but using pistachio instead of almonds.

C) For the paste:
Make the chhanno (see appendix), and mash thoroughly. Mix the ghee and milk powder. Boil the water and add sugar to make 'two taar' syrup. Add the chhanno and stir well. After 3 minutes add the milk powder and remove from heat. Allow it to cool. You now have A) Almond Sweet, B) Pistachio Sweet, and C) Paste. Arrange the two sweets on top of each other, in the round cake tin. Allow to set. Roll out the paste onto a nylon cloth. Gently lift out when ready to use. Remove from the mould and wrap the paste around this. Then decorate as described in Table No 2.
Serves 6-8.

INGREDIENTS:

1 cup (8 oz.) yoghurt
1 tbsp. gram flour
2 cups (16 oz.) mango pulp (if ready made, use 1 cup [8oz.])
3 cups water
1 tsp. salt or to taste
2 tsp. sugar
1/2 tsp. turmeric powder
1/2 tsp. ginger powder
1 tbsp. chopped ginger and chillies
1 tbsp. chopped coriander

For the seasoning (Vaghaar):
1/2 tsp. mustard seeds
1/2 tsp. cumin seeds
1/2 tsp. whole coriander seeds
A few curry leaves/bay leaves
A pinch of asafoetida
1 tbsp. ghee

9: MANGO KADHI

Mix the yoghurt, flour, mango pulp and water carefully with egg beater. Add the rest of the ingredients and bring to boil. Simmer for 10-15 minutes. Place the ghee in a small saucepan and heat. Add the seasoning ingredients. As it starts crackling, add the heated seasoning to the rest of the kadhi mixture, and allow to boil. Simmer for a further 5-10 minutes.
Serves 6-8.

INGREDIENTS:

A) **For the Spinach Gravy:**
3 tbsp. ghee and oil mixed
1 170 gm. (6 oz.) packet of
frozen creamed spinach
1 chopped onion
Salt to taste
$1/4$ tsp. ground nutmeg
$1/2$ tsp. ground pepper

B) **For the Tomato Gravy:**
450 gm. (1 lb.) boiled and
liquidized tomatoes
1 tsp. salt
$1/2$ tsp. chilli powder
1 tbsp. sugar or to taste
1 cup (8 oz.) single cream
2 tsp. cornflour mixed in $1/2$
cup (4 oz.) of water
$1/2$ cup (4 oz.) cashew nuts —
finely chopped
$1/2$ cup (4 oz.) almonds —
chopped in long strips
1 tbsp. raisins
1 small tin tomato puree

C) **For paneer balls:**
Make chhanno using 2.4 litres
(4 pints) of full cream milk
Salt to taste
$1/2$ tsp. chilli powder
1 tbsp. chopped ginger chillies
1/2 tsp. ground cloves and
cinnamon (mixed)
Oil to deep fry

D) **For Amiri Pulao:**
2 cups (16 oz.) rice
1 capsicum
Pinch of saffron
$1/2$ cup milk

10: AMIRI PULAO

A) **For the spinach gravy:**
Mix the creamed spinach (when thawed) with the onion, salt, nutmeg and pepper, and put aside.

B) **For the tomato gravy:**
Mix all the ingredients and boil for 5 minutes.

C) **For paneer balls:**
Mix all the ingredients, make balls and deep fry.

D) **Amiri Pulao**
Make the rice as normal, making sure that the rice grains are separate, not sticky. Add saffron powder, and half a cup of milk. Mix in the spinach gravy (A). Add the paneer balls (C). Heat the ghee in a saucepan, add all the above (rice and spinach) and cook gently for a few minutes. Place this mixture on an ovenproof plate. Add the tomato gravy (B) on top. Let it cook on a low heat in the oven, keeping the plate covered for about 10-15 minutes. When ready to serve decorate with rings or slices of capsicum.
Serves 8-10.

INGREDIENTS:

A) For Kofta:
Chhanno made from 1.2 litres (2 pints) of full cream milk
Ghee or oil for deep frying
1 tbsp. chopped almonds, cashew nuts and pistachio
1/4 tsp. ground cardamom
1/4 tsp. nutmeg and saffron
1 tbsp. ghee
1 tsp. khus-khus
1 tsp. ground cumin seeds (optional)
3 tbsp. breadcrumbs
6 tbsp. milk powder

B) For green sauce:
450 gm. (1 lb.) frozen peas — divide into two portions and liquidize one
1 chopped onion
3 chopped tomatoes
55 gm. (2 oz.) creamed coconut
1 tsp. salt or to taste
1 tsp. shah-jeera or cumin seed powder (optional)
1 tbsp. grated coconut (fresh or desiccated)
2 tsp. sugar
1 tsp. chilli powder
1/2 tsp. turmeric powder
3 tbsp. oil or ghee

11: GREEN GRANARY KOFTA CURRY

A) For the Kofta:
Heat the ghee and gently add the milk powder. Cook on low heat, stirring constantly. After 2 minutes remove from heat and add all the remaining ingredients except the chhanno and the breadcrumbs. Knead the chhanno thoroughly. Divide into 8-10 portions. Roll out each portion in a flat circle, using both hands to flatten. Place the mixture in the centre and roll into a ball. Complete the rest of the balls. Dip into the breadcrumbs and deep fry. Set aside.

B) For the Green sauce:
Heat the oil and fry the onions until pinkish in colour. Add the 'shah-jeera' and the tomatoes and cook thoroughly. Add salt, sugar, chilli powder, turmeric powder and creamed coconut. Put in the peas and add 1 1/2 cups of water. Let the mixture boil for 5-7 minutes, then add the koftas. Add grated coconut and coriander leaves, and remove from heat. A similar sauce can be made by using spinach instead of peas. The spinach should be boiled and liquidized.
Serves 6-8.

Puris:
See recipe number four.

INGREDIENTS:
450 gm. (1 lb.) frozen corn. Boil and divide into two portions and then mash one of the portions
225 gm (8 oz.) boiled and mashed potatoes
2 tbsp. chopped cashew nuts and dried apricots
1/2 red capsicum, finely chopped
1/2 green capsicum, finely chopped
2 celery sticks, finely chopped
1 tbsp. chopped ginger and chillies
1 tbsp. chopped coriander

12: CORN AND NUT CUTLET

Heat a tablespoon of oil in a saucepan and fry all the corn and potatoes. Add the capsicum, celery, ginger, chillies, coriander, salt and sugar and mix well. Remove from the heat and allow to cool. Once cooled, roll out into little shapes. Dip into the breadcrumbs, soaking thoroughly, and fry one by one in a shallow frying pan, turning until they turn pinkish-brown. Serve hot.
Serves 6-8.

2 tsp. sugar
Salt to taste
Juice of 1 lemon
1 cup of breadcrumbs
Oil or ghee for frying

INGREDIENTS:

1) Ingredients

1 cup (8 oz.) shelled peas
1 cup (8 oz.) finely chopped french beans
1 cup (8 oz.) finely chopped carrots
1 tin 'corn on the cob'
(chop the corn into small pieces and boil for 10 mins)
Boil the remaining vegetables.
1/2 cup (4 oz.) mixed dried fruit
450 gm. (1 lb.) grated cooking cheese
900 gm. (2 lb.) long green chillies (remove seeds and divide into vertical halves)
Take 900 gm. (2 lb.) of boiled, mashed potatoes, add salt and sugar to taste, add 1/2 tsp. garam masala, juice of 1 lemon, and 1 tbsp. ground peanuts.

2) Ingredients:

500 gm. (1 lb.) spinach lasagne. Boil as directed and divide into three equal parts. Keep aside.

3) Ingredients:

2.25 kg. (5 lb.) of liquidized tomatoes
1 tsp. red chilli powder,
Sugar and salt to taste
2 tbsp. butter
1 tbsp. cornflour
1 small tin of tomato puree

13: BAKED DISH

Stuff the chillies with the potato mixture and put aside. Coat the chillies with 2 tablespoons of oil and bake for 15 minutes. Cook the tomatoes in butter for a few minutes until boiling. Add chilli powder, sugar and salt. Once the tomato mixture starts boiling, mix the cornflour in half a cup of water and add to the tomatoes. Allow to cook for 10 minutes. Add the chopped dried fruit, remaining vegetables and tomato puree. Grease a large ovenproof dish. Layer this with one portion of the lasagne. Place half the stuffed chillies and half the vegetable mixture on top of this. Lay on another sheet of lasagne, the remaining chillies and vegetable mixture, in that order. Top with a last layer of lasagne. Cover with grated cheese, dot with butter and bake for 20 minutes. Serve hot. Serves 6-8.

INGREDIENTS:
900 gm (2 lb.) small potatoes
1 tbsp. channa flour
2 tbsp. ground peanuts
2 tbsp. sesame seeds
2 tbsp. ginger and chillies
1 tbsp. dhana-jeera
1 tbsp. brown sugar
2 tbsp. tomato puree
1 tsp. turmeric
2 tsp. chilli powder
1 tsp. lemon juice
2 tbsp. chopped coriander
1 cup oil
Salt to taste

14: JACKET POTATO CURRY

Mix all the ingredients, except the potatoes and oil, and put aside. Wash the potatoes thoroughly using a brush. Heat the oil and fry the potatoes on a low flame until tender and pinkish. When cooked, drain off half the oil (you can check the potatoes are cooked by piercing with a fork). Add all the ingredients and stir well. Cook on a low flame for 5-10 minutes. Serve hot.
Serves 6-8.

INGREDIENTS:
450 gm. (1 lb.) ground almonds
140 gm. (5 oz.) sugar
3/4 cup water
1 tbsp. ghee

15: 'BANDHINI SWEET' — ALMOND CAKE

Mix the sugar and water and heat to make 'one taar' syrup. Put the almond powder in the syrup with one tablespoon of ghee. Heat gently until it becomes a non-sticky paste (does not stick to sides of pan) and remove from heat. Allow to cool, and decorate as required.

INGREDIENTS:
2 cups (16 oz.) toovar dal
115 gm. (4 oz.) suran (root vegetable)
1 tbsp. chopped kharek (dried dates)
2 chopped medium-sized tomatoes
4-5 kokam (wash thoroughly before use)
2 tsp. salt
1 tsp. chilli powder
1/2 tsp. turmeric powder
1 tsp. dhana-jeera
1 tbsp. chopped coriander
1 tbsp. ginger and green chillies
1 tbsp. garam masala
1 tbsp. peanuts
2 tbsp. jaggery (brown sugar will do)
1 stick of ambli (tamarind seed) — soak in a cup of water and liquidize to a smooth paste.

16: DAL

Wash the dal thoroughly under running water. Soak for 1 hour, and then cook in a pressure cooker. Cut the suran into small cubes and boil it (keep aside). Add the tomatoes to the cooked dal and liquidize the mixture. Add suran to the liquidised mixture. Add the sugar, salt and all the remaining ingredients, and boil the mixture thoroughly (for at least 5-10 minutes), adding water if required. Add the chopped kharek.

For the seasoning:
Heat the oil in a metal spoon (special metallic deep spoons can be bought from most Indian shops) or small saucepan and add the rest of the ingredients to the hot oil. When sizzling, add to the cooking dal mixture.

Note: the longer the seasoned dal is allowed to simmer, the better the flavour.
Serves 6-8.

For the vaghaar (seasoning):

2 tbsp. oil	1 tsp. mustard seeds
4-5 sticks of cinnamon	1 tsp. methi seeds
4 cloves	Pinch of asafoetida

INGREDIENTS:
1 cup (8 oz.) rice
1 tsp. salt
2 tsp. sugar
2 tbsp. oil
225 gm. (8 oz.) liquidized and strained tomatoes
1/4 tsp. chilli powder

17: TOMATO RICE

Cook the rice as normal making sure that the grains are separate and not sticky. Heat the oil in a saucepan, add the remaining ingredients and allow the mixture to boil for a few minutes. Add the rice to it and cook on a low heat until all the liquid is absorbed. Serve hot.
Serves 6-8.

INGREDIENTS:
115 gm. (4 oz.) small brinjals (aubergines)
115 gm. (4 oz.) tindoras
115 gm. (4 oz.) ladies fingers
115 gm. (4 oz.) long green chillies
115 gm. (4 oz.) gunda
115 gm. (4 oz.) parwar
115 gm. (4 oz.) valor
115 gm. (4 oz.) turiya
(All these vegetables are available from Indian grocery shops.)

For the masala stuffing:
1/2 cup (4 oz.) gram flour
1/2 cup (4 oz.) roasted ground peanuts
1/2 cup (4 oz.) dhana-jeera powder
1 tbsp. chilli powder
1 tbsp. salt
3 tbsp. sugar
1 dessertspoon turmeric powder
Pinch of bicarbonate of soda
Juice of 2 lemons
2 tbsp. chopped coriander
2 tbsp. chopped ginger and chillies
4 tbsp. oil

For the seasoning:
6-7 tbsp. oil
Pinch of asafoetida
1 tsp. mustard seeds
1 tsp. cumin seeds
1/4 tsp. bicarbonate of soda

18: GREEN STUFFED VEGETABLE CURRY

Prepare all the vegetables according to their type. Steam the gunda and remove the seeds. Remove the centres of all the vegetables and stuff the masala into the prepared scored vegetables.

For the masala stuffing:
In a non-stick frying pan, roast the gram flour on a very low flame for 7 minutes. Add the remaining ingredients and mix well.

To make the curry:
Take a large ovenproof dish and arrange in it the stuffed vegetables. Arrange the vegetables in separate piles. Pour over the seasoning and cover with aluminium foil. Bake until tender. serve hot.

For the seasoning:
Heat the oil, add all the remaining seasoning ingredients. When it starts crackling, pour over the prepared vegetables.

Note: When stuffing the tooriya cut it into 5 cm. pieces. Stuff the masala between the edges of the tooriya.

For Puri:
See recipe number four.
Serves 6-8.

INGREDIENTS:

A) For the patties:
170 gm. (6 oz.) channa dal
170 gm. (6 oz.) peanuts
1 tbsp. wheatflour mixed with
a pinch of salt
6 slices of white bread
1/4 tsp. garam masala
1/2 tsp. salt
1/4 tsp. turmeric powder
1 tsp. sugar
Chilli powder to taste
1 tsp. lemon juice
Oil for frying

B) For Ragdo:
450 gm. (1 lb.) frozen corn
2 cups water
1 tbsp. cornflour
2 tbsp. chopped cashew nuts
1 tbsp. chopped capsicum
1 tbsp. chopped celery
2 tsp. sugar
1/2 tsp. salt or to taste
1/2 bunch coriander leaves
2 tsbp ground coconut, 1/2 cup
mint leaves, 1 stick ginger

C) For the chutney:
1 green capsicum
1 red capsicum
1 apple
1 tsp. salt
1/2 tsp. chilli powder
1/2 tsp. dhana-jeera
1 tsp. lemon juice
1 tbsp. jaggery or brown sugar

19: PEANUT PATTIES WITH CORN RAGDA

A) For the patties:
Soak the channa dal and peanuts separately in water overnight. Steam separately in a double boiler. Mash the cooked dal and peanuts finely (separately), preferably in a food processor. Add the salt, garam masala and turmeric powder to the ground dal. Take the bread slices and cut off the crusts. Soak the slices in water, then squeeze out by gently pressing the slices between your hands. Grind/mash these slices and mix them with the channa dal. Roll the above mixture into 10-12 balls. Grind or mash the peanuts and add salt, sugar, lemon and chilli powder to taste. Make 10-12 parts of the ground peanut and roll them into balls. Take the wheatflour, add a pinch of salt and mix it in half a cup of water. Put aside. Take each part of the channa dal mixture and press it down on your hand, making a flat circular layer. Place the peanut ball in the centre of this, and enclose it within the channa dal layer. Flatten the ball on all sides to form the shape of a patty. Dip in the wheatflour paste (prepared earlier) and deep fry. Repeat for the remaining patties.

B) For the Ragdo:
Defrost the corn. Add water to the corn and liquidize it coarsely. Place one tablespoon of cornflour in half a cup of water, and stir. Add this to the liquidized corn. Add all the remaining ingredients and boil for 10 minutes.

C) For the chutney:
Chop the capsicums and apple finely. Place in a liquidizer with the remaining ingredients and liquidize to a fine paste. Add a little lemon juice or water if required.

To serve:
Heat the patties (in a grill or microwave). Arrange them in a bowl. Add hot corn ragdo on top. Add the chutney and sprinkle with fresh coriander leaves.

INGREDIENTS:

1.8 kg. (4 lb.) Kand
450 gm. (1 lb.) potatoes
6 dessertspoons cornflour
2 tbsp. breadcrumbs
Oil for frying
Some plastic sheets

For the Chutney:
6 green chillies
1 tsp. sugar
1 tsp. lemon juice
Salt to taste
1/2 bunch coriander leaves
2 tbsp. ground coconut
1/2 cup mint leaves, 1 inch
stick of ginger

20: POTATO ROLLS WITH KAND

To make the rolls:
Boil and mash the potatoes, add salt and three dessertspoons of cornflour and mix well. Boil and mash the kand and add two dessertspoons of cornflour and salt to taste and mix well. Divide the kand mixture into three parts. Roll out one part of the potato mixture to a thickness slightly less than 1/4 inch, and apply the chutney. Roll one portion of the kand to the same thickness and place on to the rolled potatoes. Roll up the two like a swiss roll, using the plastic sheets as a base, and sprinkle breadcrumbs on it. Repeat with the remaining potato and kand mixtures. Either cut into pieces and deep fry until golden brown, or dot the roll with butter and bake in a pre-heated oven for approximately 10 minutes at moderate heat (or until pinkish). Cut into 2.5 cm. pieces and serve hot.

To make the chutney:
Mix and grind all the chutney ingredients to make a paste.
Serves 6-8.

INGREDIENTS:

A) For Daffodil flowers:
1.2 litres (2 pints) channa or paneer
3/4 cup (6 oz.) milk powder
3/4 cup (6 oz.) sugar
1 tsp. ghee
1/4 cup water
1/4 tsp. ground cardamom

B) For the base (carrot halwa):
1.5 kg. (3 lb.) carrots
3 cups (24 oz.) icing sugar
1 cup (8oz.) single cream
1 cup (8oz.) 'Carnation' milk
2 cups full cream milk
1/2 tsp. saffron
1/2 tsp. ground cardamom

C) For the Daffodil sticks (White Pumpkin Halwa):
170 gm. (6 oz.) white pumpkin
1 tsp. ghee
3/4 cup (6 oz.) icing sugar
3 cl. (1 oz.) single cream
3 cl. (1 oz.) 'Carnation' milk
2 drops of rose essence
4 drops of green food colour
1/4 tsp. ground cardamom
1/2 cup milk

21: DAFFODIL SWEET

A) Daffodil flowers:
Place the sugar and water in a saucepan, heat and make 'two taar' syrup. Mix the ghee and milk powder in a separate vessel and put aside. Mash the paneer and mix it with the syrup, stirring constantly. Maintain the heat at medium for five minutes then add the milk powder and cardamom, stir, remove from heat and allow to cool.

B) For the base (carrot halwa):
Wash and grate the carrots. Mix into them two cups of milk and cook in a saucepan over a low flame. When the milk is nearly absorbed add the 'Carnation' (condensed milk) and cream and stir, maintaining the temperature on a low flame. As it starts to thicken, add the sugar. Once the mixture becomes smooth and non-sticky, remove from heat and allow to cool.

C) For the Daffodil sticks (White Pumpkin Halwa):
Peel and grate the pumpkin. Place in a saucepan with the milk and boil at a low heat. Once the mixture thickens, add the cream and the Carnation milk. When it thickens again add the icing sugar. Cook on low heat until the mixture becomes smooth and non-sticky. Add the colour, essence and cardamom. Remove from heat and allow to cool.

INGREDIENTS:

1 tbsp. cornflour dissolved in
1-2 cups of water
Salt, sugar, lemon to taste
675 gm. (1½ lb.) frozen corn, boiled
2 tbsp. creamed coconut
2 tbsp. ghee or oil

For the paste:
3 tbsp. cashew nuts
4 green chillies
1 piece of ginger
(approximately 7 cm. long)
2 tbsp. chopped coriander
2 tbsp. desiccated coconut or fresh grated coconut
1 tbsp. poppy seeds
4 cloves
4 cinnamon sticks
5-6 whole peppercorns
1 tsp. whole coriander (seeds)
1 tsp. cummin seeds
Grind all these into a paste.

22: CORN CURRY

Liquidize a third of the corn. Heat the ghee and fry the paste for five minutes. Add the creamed coconut, salt, sugar and lemon. Add the diluted cornflour, and all the corn. Add 2-3 cups of water and boil for at least 10 minutes. Serve hot.
Serves 6-8.

INGREDIENTS:

2 cups (16 oz.) rice
2 tbsp. ghee
½ tsp. cummin seeds

For the Chutney:
6 green chillies
1 cup (8 oz.) chopped coriander leaves
½ cup (4 oz.) chopped mint
1 tsp. sugar
1 tbsp. lemon juice
1 tsp. ground cumin seeds
Salt to taste

23: CHUTNEY RICE

Wash the rice thoroughly and cook as normal, ensuring that the grains remain separate. Place aside.

For the chutney:
Rinse the chillies, coriander and mint. Mix all the ingredients and grind to a paste.

Heat the ghee, add the cumin seeds and the chutney paste. Add the cooked rice and mix well. Serve hot.
Serves 8-10.

INGREDIENTS:

1 cup (8 oz.) wholemeal flour
1 tbsp. oil
2 tsp. fennel
2 tsp. poppy seeds
Butter to brush chopda
Oil for frying
Some water to make the dough

24: CHOPDA

Add the oil to the flour and mix together gently, then gradually mix with water to make a soft dough. Knead well for a few minutes. Divide the dough into 6 equal portions and shape into balls. Roll each ball out into a circle of approximately 10 cm. in diameter. Brush each round with butter. Sprinkle the mixed fennel and poppyseed and fold in half so it forms a semicircle. Brush one side of this semicircle with butter (i.e the side facing you, not the side

For the Sprinkle
  2 tsp. sugar
  2 tsp. fennel (ground)
  2 tsp. poppy seeds
  Mix these together.

on the pastry board) and fold again so it forms a quarter circle, almost a triangular shape. Roll out the folded dough, maintaining the triangular shape, with an approximate length of 12 cm. Place the chopda on a griddle or a flat frying pan and cook. Turn over after a few seconds and brush a little oil around the edges. Cook for a few seconds further and turn again. The chopda is ready to serve when light brown on both sides. Chopdas may be prepared early and re-heated in a frying pan or microwave. If re-heating in an oven, pack them neatly and wrap in aluminium foil. If micro-waving, wrap in a kitchen towel, sprinkle with a little water and re-heat on 'defrost'.
Serves 6.

INGREDIENTS:

For the paste:
  2 dozen small adavi leaves
  3 cups (24 oz.) gram flour
  1¹/₂ cups (12 oz.) sour yoghurt
  1 tsp. garam masala
  1 tsp. bicarbonate of soda
  1 tbsp. chopped coriander leaves
  2 tbsp. chopped ginger and chillies
  1 tsp. chilli powder
  1 tsp. turmeric powder
  1 tbsp. lemon juice
  1 cup water, salt, sugar to taste
  Mix all these to a paste and then add the following ingredients, mixed, to the paste:
  2 tbsp. wheat flour
  2 tbsp. ghee

For the Vaghaar:
  4 tbsp. oil
  1 tsp. mustard seeds
  1 tsp. cumin seeds
  1 tbsp. til seeds
  ¹/₄ tsp. asafoetida
  ¹/₂ tsp. bicarbonate of soda

25: PATRA WITH GRAVY

Thoroughly wash the adavi leaves and remove the veins at the bottom of the leaves by scraping with a knife. Spread the paste evenly on to each leaf and roll into a thick cigar shape. Arrange all the rolled leaves on a large flattish ovenproof dish. Take a large deep saucepan and heat the oil. Then add all the 'vaghaar' (seasoning) ingredients. When it starts crackling add 6-7 cups of water. Allow the water to heat (not boiling) and then pour this hot seasoned water on to the rolled leaves. Cook in the oven on medium heat for at least 1 hour, until it appears cooked. Mix the left-over paste with 3 cups of water. Pour this on to the cooked patras. Place in the oven for a further 10 minutes. If the gravy becomes too thick, add more hot water. Serve hot.
Serves 6-8.

INGREDIENTS:

1 cup (8 oz.) mung dal (without husks)
1 cup (8 oz.) channa dal
1 cup (8 oz.) yoghurt
Bicarbonate of soda as required
1 tbsp. desiccated coconut
1 tbsp. coriander leaves
1 tbsp. chopped ginger and chillies
2 tbsp. oil
2 tbsp. sugar
Salt to taste

For the Vaghaar:
1/2 tsp. mustard seeds
2 tbsp. oil
1/2 tsp. cumin seeds
1 tbsp. til seeds
6-7 cups water
Foil to cover

26: MUNG AND CHANNA DAL DHOKLA

Soak the mung dal and channa dal in water overnight. In the morning, drain thoroughly, add the yoghurt, liquidize (to a crunchy paste) and leave aside for 3-4 hours in a warm place. Mix in all the remaining ingredients (except the bicarbonate of soda). Take a large saucepan and heat some water in it and place an oiled thali inside. Take 4 tablespoons of dhokla mixture, add 1/4 teaspoon of bicarbonate of soda and stir well. Place this mixture in the thali, spreading evenly. Cover the pan and cook for 7 minutes. Repeat this until all the dhokla mixture has been used. Cut the cooked dhoklas into diamond shapes and arrange on a plate. Pour the vaghaar over this. Sprinkle some desiccated coconut and coriander leaves on top.

For the vaghaar:
Heat the oil add all the remaining ingredients and, when crackling, pour over the arranged dhoklas. Serve hot.
Serves 8-10.

INGREDIENTS:

Chhanno (chopped into small pieces) made from 1.2 litres (2 pints) of full cream milk
225 gm. (8 oz.) green peas
115 gm. (4 oz.) carrots
115 gm. (4 oz.) green beans
450 gm. (1 lb.) small (baby) potatoes
115 gm. (4 oz.) cauliflower
225 gm. (8 oz.) mange-tout
225 gm. (8 oz.) cashew nuts (soak these for at least 3 hours in 1 cup of water, then liquidize)
4 large tomatoes — liquidized
1 tbsp. tomato puree
6 cinnamon sticks (small)
6 cloves
4 elaichi pods (use seeds)
1 tbsp. khus-khus
1 tbsp. dhana-jeera
1 tbsp. fennel seeds
1 tbsp. ginger and green chillies
1 tbsp. chilli sauce
2 tbsp. single cream

27: BADSHAHI VEGETABLES

Grind the cinnamon, cloves, elaichi seeds, khus-khus, dhana-jeera, and fennel seeds to a fine powder. Chop the carrots, beans, peas and cauliflower into small pieces and boil. Boil and peel the potatoes. Heat the oil, mustard seeds, coriander seeds and the ground spice mixture (cinnamon, cloves, fennel, etc. as prepared earlier). Add the tomatoes and tomato puree. Add the ginger and chillies, chilli sauce, salt, sugar, dhana-jeera and liquidized cashews and boil for 10 minutes. Roll out the Chhano, cut into square pieces, deep fry and keep aside. Add all the remaining vegetables and paneer. Boil for 10-15 minutes. Add the cream just before serving. If it becomes too thick, add half a cup of water. Serve hot.
Serves 8-10.

2 tbsp. oil
1 tbsp. ghee or butter
Salt, sugar to taste

INGREDIENTS:
340 gm. (12 oz.) pineapple
340 gm. (12 oz.) sugar
2 cups (16 oz.) milk powder
1 cup (8 oz.) chhanno
1 tbsp. ghee
A few drops of pineapple essence
150 cm. square board

INGREDIENTS:
1 cup (8 oz.) mung dal
4 cups water
1/2 tsp. turmeric powder
1 tsp. chilli powder
1 tsp. garam masala
3 finely-chopped tomatoes
1 finely-chopped onion
5 finely-chopped cloves of garlic
1 tbsp. finely-chopped coriander leaves
1 tbsp. finely-chopped ginger and chillies
1 tbsp. oil, 1/2 tsp ghee
1/2 tsp. mustard seeds
1/2 tsp. cumin seeds
Salt, sugar and lemon juice to taste

28: PINEAPPLE BARFI

Liquidize the pineapple. Add the sugar and place on medium heat for 25 minutes, keeping the pineapple boiling until it thickens. Mash the chhanno and add it to the pineapple. Stir thoroughly. Mix the ghee into the milk powder and add this to the pineapple mixture. Let it cook for a further 5 minutes, stirring constantly. Remove from the heat, add the essence and allow it to cool.
Serves 8-10.

29: MUNG DAL

Wash the dal thoroughly under running water and soak overnight, or for at least 5-6 hours. Place the dal in a saucepan with the measured quantity of water and bring to the boil. Reduce the heat and cover the pan. Allow it to simmer until the dal feels tender. Heat the oil and the ghee. Add the mustard seeds and cumin seeds and fry for 1 minute. Add the tomatoes, onion, garlic and remaining ingredients. Fry for 5 minutes. Add the dal and boil for 10 minutes. Serve hot.
Serves 6-8.

30: PARATHAS

Make the dough as in the recipe for chopda (Recipe No. 24). Divide the dough into 4-6 portions and shape into balls. Roll out each ball to form a flat circle 10 cm. in diameter. Brush each circle with butter or ghee, then fold and roll into Swiss roll shapes. Then roll out once more to form a flat circle of the same diameter. Cook this in the same way as the chopdas. Serve hot. (This can be re-heated in the same way as the chopdas.)
Serves 4-6.

INGREDIENTS:
2 cups (16 oz.) channa dal
1 cup (8 oz.) rice (broken rice
will do)
1/4 cup (2 oz.) mung dal
1/4 cup (2 oz.) urad dal
1 tbsp. chopped ginger and
chillies
1 1/2 tsp. salt or to taste
1/2 tsp. turmeric powder
Some bicarbonate of soda
2 cups (16 oz.) sour yoghurt
2 tbsp. oil
1 cup hot water

For the seasoning:
3-4 tbsp. oil
1/2 tsp. each of mustard seeds
and cumin seeds
1 tsp. til seeds (sesame seeds)

31: MIXED DAL GHOKLA

Wash all the dals and rice under running water and soak together overnight. Drain off the water, add the yoghurt and liquidize. Cover the mixture and leave aside, preferably overnight or for at least 6-7 hours, in a warm place. If mixture is too thick, add 1 cup of hot water. Boil some water in a double boiler and place an oiled thali in it. Add the salt, ginger and chillies, oil and turmeric and mix thoroughly. Take 4 tablespoons of the mixture and place in a separate vessel. Add 1/4 teaspoon of bicarbonate of soda and mix thoroughly. Place this mixture into the thali and spread evenly. Cover and cook for 10 minutes. Remove thali and repeat the procedure until all the mixture is used up. Cut the dhoklas into diamond shapes, arrange on a plate and pour the seasoning (vaghaar) on.

For the seasoning:
Heat the oil, add the remaining ingredients and when crackling, pour over the dhoklas. Serve hot.
Serves 6-8.

INGREDIENTS:
Chhanno made from 1.8 litres
(3 pints) of full cream milk
1 1/2 cups (12 oz.) boiled peas
For the mixture:
2 tbsp. chopped coriander
leaves
1 cup (8 oz.) natural yoghurt
1/2 cup (4 oz.) cream or 28 gm.
(1. oz.) creamed coconut
1 tsp. turmeric powder
3 tbsp. oil
1 tbsp. ghee
Salt to taste
Oil for frying

Roast and grind the following to a
paste:
10 red chillies
3 tsp. poppy seeds
1 tbsp. desiccated or fresh coconut
1 finely-chopped medium-
sized onion
6 cloves of garlic
10 peppercorns
6 cloves

32: PANEER AND PEA CURRY (MATTER PANEER)

Make chhanno. Knead thoroughly, then spread in a thali, chop into small pieces and deep fry. Put aside. Mix all the mixture ingredients and roast over a low heat for 15 minutes. Grind the mixture, then heat the oil and the ghee and fry for 5 minutes. Add the boiled peas, stir and allow to cook for 5 minutes, keeping the pan covered. Add the pieces of chhanno (paneer) then add the salt and the turmeric powder. Whip the yoghurt and add it to the curry. Stir and boil for a further 2-3 minutes. Add the coconut cream or fresh cream and (half a cup of boiling water, optional) serve hot.
Serves 6-8.

Note: Instead of peas you can use fresh spinach. (Chop, steam, and liquidize.) Alternatively, use frozen creamed spinach.

4 sticks cinnamon (medium
sized)
2 tbsp. fennel seeds
1 tsp cumin seeds

33: CORN CHOPS

INGREDIENTS:

450 gm. (1 lb.) potatoes —
boiled and mashed. Add 1/2
tsp. salt and 1 tsp. butter.
450 gm. (1 lb.) frozen corn —
boiled or tinned
1 chopped capsicum
1 finely-chopped celery stick
1 tbsp. chopped fresh fennel
(from Indian grocery chops)
1 tbsp. chopped ginger and
chillies
1 dessertspoon cornflour,
mixed with water
1 tsp. salt or to taste
Juice of half a lemon or to
taste
1 tsp. sugar
1 dessertspoon butter
Breadcrumbs
Oil for frying

Take the diluted cornflour and add the butter and the corn. Add capsicum, fennel, celery, salt, sugar and lemon, and heat on a low flame for 5-7 minutes. Allow to cool. Mix 1 tablespoon of cornflour in water to make a paste. Take some of the mashed potato and roll out using the palms of the hands, on to a flat circle. Place some of the corn mixture in the centre of this circle. Roll up the potato and corn into a Swiss log shape. Dip into the cornflour paste and then the breadcrumbs, and deep fry until golden brown. Repeat until all the corn and potato is used up.

34: AUBERGINES IN GRAVY

INGREDIENTS:

900 gm. (2 lb.) of small
aubergines
6 tbsp. oil
Aluminium foil for wrapping

For stuffing:
1/2 cup peas
225 gm. (8 oz.) grated carrots
1 cup (8 oz.) finely-chopped
leaf cabbage
225 gm. (8 oz.) finely-chopped
potatoes
1 tbsp. chopped ginger and
chillies
1 tbsp. dhana-jeera
1 tbsp. sugar
1 tbsp. lemon juice
1 tsp. salt
1 tsp. garam masala
2 tbsp. oil

For the gravy:
2 tbsp. ghee
2 cups (16 oz.) yoghurt
(remove all the water)
450 gm. (1 lb.) liquidized
tomatoes
Salt and sugar to taste

Boil the peas. Heat some oil in a frying pan and add the potatoes. When the potatoes are cooked, add the rest of the ingredients for the stuffing and stir well. Remove from heat and put aside. Wash the aubergines and cut off the stalks. Make a vertical slit in the centre of each and fill with the stuffing. Arrange the stuffed aubergines on an ovenproof plate. Heat the rest of the oil and pour over the aubergines. Cover with foil and cook on medium heat (in the oven) for at least 1 hour or until cooked.

For the gravy:
Heat the ghee. Add the masala paste. Add the tomatoes and simmer on a low heat for 10 minutes. Add the yoghurt, salt and ginger and remove from heat. When ready to serve, pour the gravy over the cooked aubergines, cover again with foil and bake in the oven for a further 10 minutes. Serve hot.
Serves 8-10.

Grind the following into a paste:

1 chopped onion	1/2 tsp. turmeric powder
6 cloves of garlic	3 cinnamon sticks
1 stick ginger (approximately 8 cm. long)	3 cloves
2 tbsp. desiccated coconut	6 peppercorns
6 green chillies	1 tsp. khus-khus
1 tsp. chilli powder	1/2 tsp. coriander seeds
	1 tbsp. dhana-jeera

INGREDIENTS:
115 gm. (4 oz.) beans
115 gm. (4 oz.) carrots
115 gm. (4 oz.) potatoes
3 sing pieces (Saragava sing)
1/4 cup (2 oz.) peas
1 turnip
2 tomatoes
1 banana
1 tbsp. gram flour
1 tbsp. cashew nuts
1 tbsp. chopped dried apricots
1/2 tbsp. raisins
115 gm. (4 oz.) creamed coconut
2 tbsp. chopped ginger and chillies
2 tbsp. chopped coriander leaves
1/2 tsp. chilli powder
1/2 tsp. turmeric powder
1 1/2 cups (12 oz.) natural yoghurt
2 tsp. dhana-jeera powder

For the seasoning:
1/2 tsp. mustard seeds
1/2 tsp. cummin seeds
1 tsp. dhana seeds
5 cloves
3 cinnamon sticks
2 tsp. dhana-jeera powder
A few curry leaves and bay leaves
Pinch of asafoetida
2 tbsp. ghee
Salt and sugar to taste

35: NAVRATNA KADHI

Chop the sing pieces and boil together with the green peas. Chop the beans, carrots and potatoes. Place one tablespoon ghee in a pan and fry the beans, carrots and potatoes. When cooked, add the peas, sing and bananas (chopped round). Mix the yoghurt and the gram flour thoroughly, adding 2 cups of water. Add the salt, sugar, ginger and chillies, dhana-jeera powder, turmeric and chilli powder. Add this to the cooked vegetables and boil together. Keep stirring regularly. Heat the rest of the ghee in a separate pan. Add mustard and cumin seeds, dhana seeds, cloves, cinnamon, asafoetida, bay and curry leaves. When crackling, add this to the boiling kadhi. Add fresh coriander leaves, cashew nuts, apricots, raisins and boil again. Serve hot.
Serves 8-10.

INGREDIENTS:
1 cup (8 oz.) mung dal
450 gm. (1 lb.) ghee
1 1/4 cups (10 oz.) sugar
1.2 litres (2 pints) milk
1/4 tsp. saffron
1/2 tsp. ground cardamom

36: MUNG DAL SWEET

Wash the dal thoroughly under running water. Soak overnight (for at least 12 hours). Drain the water and liquidize finely. Heat the ghee in a saucepan. Add the mung dal and cook on a very low (roast) heat, stir continuously. (It will take almost 2 hours to cook.) When it becomes pinkish in colour, add the milk and allow it to cook until it thickens and all the milk is absorbed. Add the sugar and continue to cook, stirring constantly. Once the ghee starts to separate, remove from heat and add the saffron and cardamom.

37: COCONUT RICE

INGREDIENTS:

2 cups (16 oz.) of rice
2 tbsp. ghee
115 gm. (4 oz.) creamed
coconut
3 bay leaves
1/2 tsp. cardamom seeds
4 cinnamon sticks
4 cloves

Wash the rice under running water and drain. Heat ghee and add the cloves, cinnamon, bay leaves, and cardamom. Add the rice and fry for a few minutes. Add the creamed coconut, salt and water and continue to cook the rice.
Serves 8-10.

38: NAAN

INGREDIENTS:

450 gm. (1 lb.) plain flour (use strong white flour)
1 tsp. dry instant yeast
1 tsp. salt
3 tbsp. oil
3 tbsp. natural yoghurt
1 tsp. sugar
Butter or oil for frying
Lukewarm water

For Peshawari Naan:
1 tbsp. chopped nuts
1 tsp. ground fennel
1 tsp. poppy seeds

Mix the sugar, salt, yeast and oil in the flour and mix together gently. Add the water to make a soft dough. Knead thoroughly for 5-10 minutes. Place the dough in a large airtight vessel at room temperature and leave untouched until it doubles in size. Knead thoroughly again and leave at the same temperature, and in the same vessel, for 6-7 hours. Then divide the dough into equal portions. Take one portion and roll into an oblong shape and bake both sides, under the grill. Dot with butter and serve hot.

Variations: These naans can be stuffed with nuts to make a Peshawari Naan. Mix chopped nuts, ground fennel and poppy seeds together, roll into a ball and place in the centre of the dough. Fold over the dough then roll out again in an oblong shape.

39: MOGHLAI POTATO CURRY

INGREDIENTS:

450 gm. (1 lb.) small potatoes
450 gm. (1 lb.) boiled or frozen peas
4 tbsp. cooking oil for frying
49.5 gm. 1/4 packet of creamed coconut
1 tbsp. cornflour
1 small tin of tomato puree
1 tbsp. ground chillies and ginger
1 tbsp. chopped parsley or coriander
Few bay leaves
Oil to deep fry potatoes
Sugar and salt to taste
1 tbsp. chopped cashew nuts
1 tbsp. ground cashew nuts
1 tbsp. chopped peanuts
1 tbsp. ground peanuts
1/2 tsp. turmeric powder
1 tsp. chilli powder

Roast all the paste ingredients over a low flame for 10 minutes, then grind together. Boil the potatoes, peel and deep fry. Prick the potatoes with a fork to make holes in them and put aside. Chop and liquidize the tomatoes. Heat the oil in a pan and fry the asafoetida, bay leaves, cashew nuts, peanuts, chillies and ginger, and chopped coriander for 5 minutes. Add the liquidized tomatoes, tomato puree and creamed coconut. Boil for a few minutes. Add the potatoes, peas, sugar and salt to taste. Add a 1/2 teaspoon of turmeric powder and the chilli powder and boil for 10-15 minutes. Serve hot.
Serves 8-10.

For the paste:
1 cup (8 oz.) grated or desiccated coconut
1 dessertspoon coriander seeds
1 tsp. cumin seeds
10 pieces cardamom
1 dessertspoon poppy seeds

1/2 tsp. cloves
1/2 tsp. pepper
1/2 tsp. cinnamon
1 dessertspoon fennel seeds
1 dessertspoon sesame seeds
1/2 tsp. javantri
1/2 tsp. nutmeg
Pinch of asafoetida

INGREDIENTS:

450 gm. (1 lb.) potatoes
450 gm. (1 lb.) frozen corn
2 tbsp. cornflour
2 tbsp. rice flour
1/2 cup water
Green chutney (See recipe 23)
1 tbsp. butter and cooking oil
Salt and sugar to taste
1 capsicum, chopped
1 stick celery, chopped

40: SWEET CORN ROLLS

Cook the corn in a little water. Make a white sauce using the cornflour, butter and water. Add this to the cooked corn, cook over a high flame and stir gently. Add the salt, capsicum and celery. Remove from heat and allow to cool. Cook and mash the potatoes and add the green chutney. Heat a dessertspoon of oil and add the potato mixture. Cook for 5 minutes, stirring constantly. Remove from the heat and allow to cool. Sprinkle some rice flour on a flat surface and roll out the potato mixture. Spread the cooked corn on top of it. Roll up like a Swiss roll. Either cut carefully into pieces of about 1-2 cm. thickness and deep fry until golden brown or bake the roll in an oven at moderate temperature after brushing a little butter over it. Serve by cutting into 2 cm. pieces while hot and garnish with chutney.
Serves 2-4.

INGREDIENTS:

2 cups (16 oz.) rice
1/2 cup (4 oz.) toovar dal
1/2 cup (4 oz.) channa dal
1/2 cup (4 oz.) mung dal
1/2 cup (4 oz.) urad dal
1/2 cup (4 oz.) wheat
1/2 cup (4 oz.) joovar
2 cups (16 oz.) yoghurt
2 tsp. chilli powder
1/2 tsp. turmeric powder
Salt to taste
4 tbsp. golkeri — an Indian pickle (available from Indian shops)
4 tbsp. oil
1/2 tsp. bicarbonate of soda

41: DAMLI DHOKLA

Wash the rice and soak in clean water overnight. Wash the dals and soak overnight. Drain the rice and grind to a paste. Drain the dals, add yoghurt and grind to a paste. Mix the two pastes and place the mixture in a warm place (room temperature). Keep covered and untouched for 6 hours. Add salt, pickles, chilli powder, chillies, turmeric powder and mix thoroughly. Add 4 tablespoons of oil and 1 2 a teaspoon of bicarbonate of soda. Heat some water in a large saucepan. Take some of the mixture and place in an 'idli maker' or small bowls. Place these inside the vessel so that the mixture cooks in steam. Cook for 10 minutes. Repeat until all the mixture is used. These dhoklas can be made in advance and heated in a microwave oven on 'defrost' for 5 minutes. Serve hot with oil.
Serves 6-8.

INGREDIENTS:

Chhanno made from 2.4 litres (4 pints) of full cream milk
3/4 cup (6 oz.) sugar and 1/2 cup water
1/2 cup (4 oz.) milk powder
1 tbsp. ghee
1/2 tsp. ground cardamom
1 tbsp. chopped pistachio and almond nuts (mixed)

42: DAISY SWEET

Mash the chhanno and knead thoroughly. Gently mix the ghee with the milk powder. Add the chhanno and mix thoroughly. After 5 minutes add the milk powder. Continue cooking and stirring for a further 2 minutes. Add the chopped nuts and remove from heat. Place in a cake mould and refrigerate for 20 minutes.
Serves 10-12.

INGREDIENTS:

1 cup (8 oz.) rice
¼ cup (2 oz.) boiled green toovar
115 gm. (4 oz.) brinjal (very small)
½ tsp. salt
½ tsp. sugar
¼ tsp. turmeric powder
1 tsp. lemon juice
1 tbsp. butter
55 gm. (2 oz.) creamed coconut
Foil
Ovenproof serving dish

For the stuffing:

1 tsp. gram flour
1 tsp. grated coconut
1 tsp. chopped ginger and chillies
½ tsp. chilli powder
1 tsp. dhana-jeera
¼ tsp. turmeric powder
1 tsp. oil
1 tsp. sugar
1 tsp. lemon juice
Oil for frying the brinjals
Salt to taste

INGREDIENTS:

600 ml. (1 pint) natural yoghurt
1 tbsp. gram flour
1 tbsp. chopped ginger and chillies
1 tbsp. sugar
1 tsp. salt
½ tsp. turmeric powder
1 tsp. ground dhana-jeera
300 ml. (½ pint) water

For vaghaar (seasoning):

1 tbsp. ghee or oil
½ tsp. mustard seeds
1 tsp. cumin seeds
½ tsp. whole coriander seeds
½ tsp. fenugreek seeds
Pinch of asafoetida
Few curry leaves

43: BRINJAL AND TOOVAR PULLAO

Mix all the ingredients for the stuffing together, and stuff the brinjals. Heat some oil in a saucepan and fry them over a low flame, keeping the pan covered. Cook until tender, then add the boiled toovar, sugar, salt, lemon, turmeric and chilli powder. Boil the rice and add the salt. Add butter and coconut cream. Mix the toovar/brinjal mixture into the rice. Grease an ovenproof dish and place the rice in it. Cover with foil and bake in a pre-heated oven on high for 15 minutes. Serve hot.
Serves 5-6.

44: KADHI

Mix the gram flour, the water and the yoghurt, using a whisk or an egg beater. Add the rest of the ingredients and boil for 10-15 minutes, stirring occasionally. Heat the ghee (for the seasoning) and add the rest of the ingredients. When crackling pour the seasoning over the kadhi. Serve hot.
Serves 4-6.

INGREDIENTS:

900 gm. (2 lb.) small round potatoes

450 gm. (1 lb.) chopped tomatoes

Oil for frying

For the paste:

3 onions

1/2 fresh coconut (grated) or 1 cup (8 oz.) of desiccated

3 tbsp. peanuts

1 tbsp. oil

2 tsp. whole coriander seeds

1 tsp. cumin seeds

1 tbsp. chopped ginger and chillies

1 tbsp. fresh coriander leaves, chopped

1 tbsp. sesame seeds

For the rest of the curry:

Salt and sugar to taste

Juice of 1 lemon

1 tsp. chilli powder

1 tsp. garam masala

2 cups (16 oz.) natural yoghurt (thoroughly whisked)

1 tbsp. oil

1 tsp. turmeric

45: PUNJABI POTATO CURRY

Boil the potatoes, then peel and fry them. Prick holes in them with a fork and put aside. Grind all the ingredients for the paste and put aside. Heat the oil and fry the tomatoes for 5 minutes. Add the paste and cook for a further 10 minutes. Add the rest of the ingredients for the curry. Then add the fried potatoes and boil the curry for 5 minutes. Serve hot.
Serves 4-6.

Masala Naan:
Make the naan as in Recipe No. 38. Stuff with spiced green peppers or spiced mashed potatoes.

Spices for Masala Naan:

1 tsp. chilli powder

1/2 tsp. salt

1 tbsp. lemon juice

1 tsp. sugar

INGREDIENTS:

20 small adavi leaves

1/2 cup (8 oz.) gram flour

1/2 cup (8 oz.) dhokra flour

1/2 cup (8 oz.) yellow corn flour

1 tbsp. grated coconut

2 tbsp. ground peanuts

1 tbsp. sesame seeds

1 tbsp. ground ginger and chillies

2 cups (16 oz.) natural yoghurt

1 tbsp. chopped fresh coriander

Lemon, salt and sugar to taste

225 gm. (8 oz.) frozen corn

1/2 tsp. bicarbonate of soda

1/2 tsp. ground cinnamon and cloves (mixed)

2 tbsp. ghee

1 tbsp. wheatflour

46: PATRA (ADAVI LEAVES) SAMOSAS

Wash the adavi leaves and remove the veins on either side by scraping with a knife. Cut the leaves into two parts. Mix all the ingredients together except the ghee, wheatflour and gravy ingredients to make a thick paste. Heat the ghee and wheatflour and mix them, then add the paste. Remove from heat. Spread the paste thinly on one side of the adavi leaf and fold it into a samosa shape (with the paste inside). Repeat until all the leaves have been used. Steam these by placing on a strainer in an enclosed pan or in a pressure cooker for at least an hour. Check if the leaves are tender and cook for longer, if required. Remove from heat and allow the samosas to cool.

To make the gravy:
Heat the oil, add the creamed coconut and the rest of the ingredients, and boil for 7 minutes. Add the prepared samosas to the gravy and boil again until the gravy thickens. Serve hot.
Serves 4-6.

For the gravy:
1 tbsp. oil
99 gm. (3¹/₂ oz.) creamed
coconut
Salt, sugar, lemon, chilli
powder to taste

INGREDIENTS:
900 gm. (2 lb.) tooriya
5 tbsp. oil
1 tsp. mustard seeds
Pinch of asafoetida

For the masala:
2 tbsp. gram flour
2 tbsp. ground peanuts
1 tbsp. sesame seeds (powdered)
1 tbsp. dhana-jeera
1 tbsp. sugar
1 tsp. turmeric powder
1 tsp. salt (or to taste)
2 tbsp. tomato puree
1 tbsp. cooking oil
1 tbsp. chopped ginger and
chillies
1 tbsp. chopped coriander
Mix all these ingredients
together and keep aside.

47: GREEN TOORIYA CURRY

Wash and prepare the tooriya. Cut into pieces approximately 4 cm. long, and then cut vertical slits in each piece. Heat the oil, add the mustard seeds and asafoetida and when crackling add the tooriya. Allow the tooriya to cook in a covered pan on low heat until tender. Stir while cooking. When cooked, add the masala, stir well and allow to cook on a medium heat for a further 10 minutes.
Serves 8-10.

INGREDIENTS:
Part 1:
900 gm. (2 lb.) stoned dates
1 tbsp. ghee

Part 2:
450 gm. (1 lb.) desiccated
coconut
225 gm. (8 oz.) sugar
1 large carton double cream
¹/₂ tsp. cardamom powder
A few drops of pink food colour

48: ROYAL CAKE

Part 1:
Place a tablespoon of ghee in a frying pan and fry the dates on low heat. Cook until they do not stick to the sides of the pan. Remove from the heat and allow to cool. Divide the dates into 3 portions.

Part 2:
Mix the coconut, cream and sugar. Heat on low until the mixture does not stick to the sides of the pan. Remove from heat, add the pink colour and cardamom. Divide into 2 portions and allow to cool.

Part 3:
    225 gm. (8 oz.) grated mava
    2 dessertspoons ghee
    1 tbsp. poppy seeds
    1 tbsp. ground fennel seeds
    3/4 cup (6 oz.) caster sugar
    1 tsp. ground cardamom seeds
    1/2 tsp. ground nutmeg
    1/2 tsp. ground saffron
    3 tbsp. ground almonds
    3 tbsp. ground pistachio nuts

Part 4:
    Marzipan for decoration
    Pink and green food colour
    1 round ovenproof dish (11"
    in diameter)
    Buttered paper or baking
    paper
    Aluminium foil

Part 3:
Heat the ghee and fry the mava for 10 minutes on a low heat. Mix the remainder of the ingredients (Part 2) and allow to cool.

Part 4:
Cut the foil into a round shape which should be at least three times the diameter of the serving dish, and place it at the bottom of the dish. Take one part of the date mixture (Part 1) and roll it out to form a thick layer. Place this layer on the foil. Spread out part of the coconut mixture (Part 2) on top of the date layer. Take the mava mixture (Part 3) and layer this on top of the coconut mixture. Add the second part of the coconut mixture. Take the second portion of the date mixture (Part 1) and place this on top of the mava mixture. Finally cut strips of the last portion of the date mixture, (Part 1) and cover the sides of the cake with it. Tidy all the edges of the cake and seal them with the date mixture. You may find it easier to use a cake ring. Mix some pink and some green colour separately in a little marzipan. Make green marzipan leaves and pink flowers to decorate the cake.

INGREDIENTS:
    1/2 cup (4 oz.) channa dal
    1/2 cup (4 oz.) mung dal
    (split)
    3/4 cup (6 oz.) toovar dal
    1/4 cup (2 oz.) masoor dal
    1/4 cup (2 oz.) urad
    2 tsp. salt or to taste

Masala for paste:
    1 tbsp. coriander seeds
    1 tsp. cumin seeds
    7-8 red chillies
    1 tbsp. chopped ginger and
    chillies
    6-7 cloves of garlic
    4 sticks of cinnamon
    6 cloves
    6 whole peppercorns
    2 chopped onions (medium
    sized)
    2 tbsp. chopped coriander
    Grind these into a paste.

49: PANCHKUTI DAL

Wash all the dals under running water and soak for an hour. Cook in a pressure cooker with 6-7 cups of water. Heat the ghee and oil and fry the masala for 5 minutes. Add the chopped tomatoes and fry for a few minutes further. Add the cooked dal, turmeric powder, salt, jaggery and lemon juice. Boil for 10-12 minutes. Serves 10-12.

For the rest of the dal:
    2 tbsp. oil
    1 tbsp. ghee
    2 tbsp. jaggery or brown sugar
    Juice of 1 lemon
    4 large, finely-chopped tomatoes
    1/4 tsp. turmeric powder

INGREDIENTS:

450 gm. (1 lb.) plain flour (use strong white flour)
1 tsp. dry instant yeast
1 tsp. salt
3 tbsp. oil
3 tbsp. natural yoghurt
1 tsp. sugar
Butter or oil for frying
Lukewarm water

50: KULCHA

Mix the sugar, salt, yeast and oil in the flour and mix together gently. Add water to make a soft dough. Knead thoroughly for 5-10 minutes. Place the dough in a large airtight vessel at room temperature and leave aside until it doubles in size. Knead again thoroughly and leave at the same temperature, and in the same vessel, for 6-7 hours. Divide the dough into equal portions. Take one portion and roll out into a round shape. Fry both sides (in the same way as the parathas, Recipe No. 30).
Serves 5-6.

Variations: Stuffed Kulcha.
Make a stuffing as in Recipe No. 30. Stuff inside the dough in the same way as for the parathas and fry both sides. A stuffing of finely chopped dried fruits and nuts also makes a delicious combination.

INGREDIENTS:

2 cups (16 oz.) mung dal
3 tbsp. oil
450 gm. (1lb.) white flour
1 tsp. cumin seeds
2 tbsp. tamarind powder or lemon juice
1 tsp. chilli powder
1 tsp. of cinnamon, cloves, pepper (mixed)
Pinch of asafoetida
Salt to taste, a
pinch of black salt
2 tbsp. oil
3 tbsp. ghee
1 tbsp. chopped ginger and chillies
1 tbsp. chopped coriander leaves
Oil for frying

For the chutney:
2 tbsp. tamarind
1 packet (250 gm.) dates
1 tsp. salt
1 tsp. cumin powder
1 tsp. chilli powder
Yoghurt to serve

51: KHASTA KACHORI

Soak the mung dal for 5-7 hours after cleaning. Grind the mung dal finely. Heat 2 tablespoons of oil in a frying pan and add the cumin seeds and asafoetida. When crackling, add the mung dal. Cook on a low heat for 15 minutes. Remove from the heat and add salt, cloves, cinnamon, pepper, chilli powder, tamarind powder, black salt, ginger and chillies and coriander leaves and mix thoroughly. (The mixture should be fairly dry.) Leave the mixture aside. Add 3 tablespoons of ghee, add a little salt to taste to the flour and make a uniform dough with water. Knead thoroughly. Divide the dough into small balls (making sure they are all the same size). This dough should make 20-25 balls. Take the dough balls and flatten into circles. Place the mung dal balls in the centre of the dough circles and close up. Smooth the edges of the balls to give a rounded shape. Heat some oil in a deep frying pan. Remove from heat and allow to cool for a few minutes. Place the kachories in the oil and return the pan to the heat. Fry the kachories until they puff up (similar to puris) and turn pinkish in colour. (This should take half an hour).

For the chutney:
Soak the dates and tamarind in 2 cups of water, liquidize and strain. Add the salt, chilli powder and jeera (cumin) powder.

For the garnish:
Soak some Mung dal overnight until it sprouts. Steam and keep aside.

To serve:
Pierce the kachories to make a hole, place the mung sprouts in this, pour over yoghurt and chutney, and sprinkle chilli powder and jeera (cumin) powder on top.

Note: It is easier if the mung dal mixture is also divided into equal parts before folding into the pastry.
Serves 10-12.

INGREDIENTS:

2.25 kg. (5 lb.) green papadi (available from any Indian grocery shop)
450 gm. (1 lb.) sweet potatoes
6-7 bananas
900 gm. (2 lb.) kund (pinkish in colour)
2 cups cooking oil
2 cups milk
450 gm. (1 lb.) small aubergines
900 gm. (2 lb.) small potatoes
1/2 tsp. bicarbonate of soda

For the Masala:

3 grated coconuts
2 bunches of coriander leaves, finely-chopped (to measure 1 1/2 cups)
900 gm. (2 lb.) frozen green toovar (boiled and mashed)
1/2 tsp. bicarbonate of soda
3 tsp. salt
1/2 tsp. asafoetida
2 tbsp. chopped ginger and chillies
7-8 cloves of garlic, ground
5-6 tsp. sugar
Mix well and put aside.

For the Muthias (flour balls):

3 cups (24 oz.) wheatflour
1 cup (8 oz.) gram flour
1 bunch chopped fenugreek (methi leaves) (to measure 1/2 cup)
1 tsp. salt or to taste
1 tbsp. chopped ginger and chillies
1 tsp. sugar
1/2 tsp. red chilli powder
Pinch of asafoetida
4 tbsp. oil
1/2 tsp. turmeric powder
Oil for deep frying

52: SURTI UNDHYU

First prepare the flour balls. Mix the flour, oil and remainder of the ingredients thoroughly. Divide the mixture into small balls, roll them into oblong shapes, and deep fry. Put aside. Wash all the vegetables thoroughly. Wash the papadi and kund. Cut the kund and sweet potatoes into square shapes. Cut slits in the centre of the potatoes and aubergines. Stuff all the vegetables with the masala. Chop the bananas into small pieces and make slits. If there is any masala left over (after vegetables are used up) put it aside. In a large vessel, add oil, 2 cups of water, and 1/2 teaspoon of bicarbonate of soda and boil. Add 3 teaspoons of salt. Add the papadi and boil for 10 minutes. Add the kund and sweet potatoes and boil for 10 minutes. Then place the remaining masala in the mixture. After a few minutes place the potatoes and aubergines in the boiling mixture and cook on a low heat. (Keep the pan covered.) Place a steel plate on top of the covered pan with some water in the plate (use a steel thali). After approximately half an hour, when the potatoes are cooked, place the flour balls and bananas in the mixture. Remove excess water and cook for 20 minutes on a low flame. Add 2 cups of milk and cook on a low heat for a further 10 minutes.

Serves 10-15.

Note: If you cannot get papadi use valor (green vegetables). By adding the milk at the last stage the curry will remain liquid and will not dry up.

INGREDIENTS:
   1 cup (8 oz.) channa dal
   2 tbsp. natural yoghurt
   1 cup (8 oz.) puffed rice
   (pawa)
   1 tbsp. chopped ginger and
   chillies
   1 tbsp. coriander leaves
   1 tsp. salt
   1 tbsp. oil
   Bicarbonate of soda
   Oil to brush the thali
   1/4 tsp. turmeric powder

For the seasoning:
   2 tbsp. oil
   1/2 tsp. mustard seeds
   1/2 tsp. cumin
   1 tsp. sesame seeds
   Pinch of asafoetida

53: PUFFED RICE DHOKLA

Wash the channa dal and allow to soak overnight. Drain. Add the yoghurt and liquidize the mixture. Soak the puffed rice for 3-4 hours, then mash thoroughly. Mix all the ingredients together thoroughly (including the channa dal and the puffed rice) except the bicarbonate of soda. Take a large vessel, fill a quarter full with water and heat. Take a medium sized thali, brush it with oil and place it on top of the heating vessel (the thali will be warmed by the steam). Take 3 tablespoons of the dhokla mixture in a bowl, add 1/4 teaspoon of the bicarbonate of soda and mix thoroughly. Pour the mixture into the heated thali. Place the thali back on top of the vessel and cover. Cook for 10 minutes. Remove from heat, cut into diamond shapes and serve hot.

Variations: The prepared dhoklas can be seasoned. Heat oil, add rest of the ingredients and, when crackling, pour over the prepared dhoklas.
Serves 4-6.

INGREDIENTS:
   Chhanno made from 2.4 litres
   (4 pints) of full cream milk
   (red top)
   1 flower-shaped mould or
   cake tin
   1 1/2 cups (12 oz.) tinned
   mango pulp
   1 1/2 cups (12 oz.) sugar
   2 cups (16 oz.) milk powder
   1/2 cup (4 oz.) single cream
   1 tbsp. chopped almonds and
   pistachios
   (If using fresh mango pulp,
   add 2 cups [16 oz.] sugar)

54: MANGO SWEET

Put the sugar into the mango pulp and boil together on medium heat for at least 15 minutes. Add the chhanno (after kneading thoroughly) and heat again for 10 minutes, stirring constantly. Once the mixture thickens, remove from heat and add the chopped nuts. Mix the milk powder into the cream and add this to the mixture. Cook for a further 5 minutes. Grease the mould or cake tin and place the mango sweet in it. Allow to set. Then invert the set sweet on to a serving plate and decorate with sugar flowers and chocolate icing or spread.
Serves 8-10.

INGREDIENTS:

1/2 cup (4 oz.) toovar dal
4 cups (32 oz.) buttermilk
1 dessertspoon gram flour
1 turnip (finely chopped)
1 potato (finely chopped)
6 sticks of sing (Saragwa)
1 aubergine (finely chopped)
2 tomatoes chopped
25 gm. (1 oz.) guwaar chopped
6 ladies fingers chopped
1 tbsp. chopped ginger and chillies
1 tbsp. chopped coriander leaves
1 tsp. salt, 1/2 tsp. chilli powder, 1/2 tsp. turmeric, 1 tsp. dhana-jeera, mixed together

For the seasoning:
1 tbsp. ghee
4 cloves
4 sticks of cinnamon
Pinch of asafoetida
A few bay leaves and curry leaves
1/4 tsp. methi seeds
1/4 tsp. coriander seeds
1/4 tsp. mustard seeds
1/4 tsp. cumin seeds

55: BHATIYA KADHI

Wash the dal and cook in a pressure cooker (with 1 cup of water). Cut the sing, trim the guwaar and place in the cooker with the dal. Mix the channa flour with the buttermilk using whisk. Once the dal is cooked, add the gram flour, buttermilk, the remaining vegetables and remaining ingredients (except the ones for the seasoning) and tomatoes and allow to boil for at least 15 minutes.

For the seasoning:
Heat the ghee, add the rest of the ingredients and, when crackling, pour into the boiling kadhi. Cook for a further 5-10 minutes. Serve hot. Garnish with coriander leaves.
Serves 4-6.

INGREDIENTS:

225 gm. (8 oz.) shelled peas
225 gm. (8 oz.) carrots — cut into small round pieces
225 gm. (8 oz.) cauliflower cut into small pieces
2 tsp. sugar
juice of 1 lemon
1/2 tsp. chilli powder
1/2 tsp. turmeric
1/2 tsp. garam masala
2 tsp. dhana-jeera
Pinch of bicarbonate of soda
Salt to taste
1 chopped onion, 2 chopped tomatoes
1 tbsp. chopped ginger and chillies

56: MIXED VEGETABLE CURRY

Heat the oil and add the rest of the seasoning ingredients. Add the peas and cook on a low heat for a few minutes. Add 1/4 cup of water and the bicarbonate of soda. When the peas are half cooked, add the rest of the ingredients, cook (uncovered) and stir occasionally. All the water should be fully absorbed. Serve hot.
Serves 4.

1 tbsp. chopped coriander
leaves

For the seasoning:
6 tbsp. oil
$1/2$ tsp. mustard seeds
$1/2$ tsp. cumin seeds
Pinch of asafoetida

INGREDIENTS :

For the stuffing:
450 gm. (1 lb.) boiled mashed
potatoes
$1/2$ cup (4 oz.) boiled mashed
peas
$1/2$ cup (4 oz.) grated carrots
1 tsp. garam masala
Salt, sugar and lemon juice to
taste
1 tbsp. chopped ginger and
chillies
1 dessertspoon sesame seeds
1 tbsp. oil
1 tsbp chopped coriander

57: STUFFED PARATHAS

See the basic recipe (Recipe No. 30) and prepare the dough. Heat the oil, fry the sesame seeds, peas, carrots and remaining ingredients. Mix well, remove from heat and allow to cool. Divide into 10-12 portions. Roll out the prepared dough. Place a portion of the stuffing in the centre of the dough circle. Fold over and seal. Roll out again to make a thick circle 16 cm. in diameter. Heat the frying pan and grease it generously with oil. Cook the paratha on one side, spread some oil on the side facing you and turn it over. Then cook the second side. Repeat until all the parathas are done. Serve hot.
Serves 10-12.

INGREDIENTS:

900 gm. (2 lb.) potatoes —
boiled and mashed
1 tsp. salt
$1/2$ tsp. lemon juice
1 tsp. cornflour and 4 slices of
white bread, soaked in water,
squeezed dry and mixed with
the potatoes
Mix all the above together.
450 gm. (1 lb.) frozen corn —
ready cooked
2 tbsp. chopped peanuts
1 tbsp. sesame seeds
1 tbsp. chopped ginger and
chillies
1 chopped cucumber
(drained)
1 tbsp. chopped coriander
leaves
$1/2$ tsp. chilli powder
2 tsp. salt or to taste
1 tsp. sugar
Juice of $1/2$ a lemon
Oil to fry

58: CORN PATTIES

Mix the corn, chopped peanuts, sesame seeds, chopped ginger and chillies, chopped (drained) cucumber, chopped coriander leaves, chilli powder, salt, sugar and lemon juice together. Take a portion of the potato in your hand and flatten into a round shape. Place a ball of corn mixture in the centre of this. Fold over and shape into a sausage. Repeat until all the potato and corn mixture is used up. Deep fry until golden brown in colour. Serve hot.
Serves 4-6.

INGREDIENTS:
> 450 gm. (1 lb.) potatoes —
> boiled, peeled and chopped
> into small cubes.
> 3 tbsp. oil
> 1 tbsp. sesame seeds
> 1 tbsp. cumin seeds

For the chutney:
> 1 cup (8 oz.) chopped
> coriander leaves
> 6 green chillies
> 1 cooking apple
> 1 tbsp. chopped peanuts
> 1 tsp. cumin seeds
> 1 tsp. salt
> 2 tsp. sugar
> Juice of 1/2 lemon

59: POTATO CURRY WITH GREEN CHUTNEY

Mix all the chutney ingredients to make a thin paste. Cover the potatoes with the chutney. Heat the oil and add the sesame and cumin seeds. When crackling, add the chutneyed potatoes and cook on a medium heat for 5-7 minutes. Serve hot. Serves 4-6.

INGREDIENTS:
> 2.25 kg. (5 lb.) potatoes
> 450 gm. (1 lb.) frozen corn
> 1 tsp. salt
> 1 tbsp. butter

For the Corn mixture:
> 2 tbsp. cornflour
> 1/2 cup water
> 2 tbsp. ground peanuts
> 2 tbsp. chopped mixed dried
> fruits and nuts (almonds,
> cashews, nutmeg, dried
> apricots, apples, dates, etc.)
> 1 dessertspoon raisins
> 1 dessertspoon sesame seeds
> 1 tbsp. butter
> 1 tbsp. ground ginger and
> chillies
> 1 cake tin (non-stick) 22 cm.
> in diameter
> 2 tsp. sugar or to taste
> Juice of 1 lemon
> 2 tbsp. chopped coriander
> leaves

For the chutney:
> 6 green chillies
> 25 gm. (1 oz.) coriander leaves
> 1 tsp. salt
> 1 tsp. sugar

60: POTATO CAKE

Boil the peas and liquidize with a tablespoon of water. Add butter and salt and keep aside. Boil the potatoes, peel, mash and add salt and butter. Divide the potato mixture into 4 parts. Mix in the corn mixture and cook for 10 minutes: Add the dried fruits, salt (to taste), lemon juice, chillies and ginger, coriander, sesame seeds and peanuts and stir well. Mix the water and cornflour and add this to the corn mixture. Cook on low for 10 minutes, stirring continuously. Remove from heat and divide mixture into two parts. Grease the cake tin. Roll out one portion of the potato mixture and place this at the bottom of the tin. Roll out a second portion and spread this round the inner sides of the cake tin. Spread the chutney on the potato both at the base of the tin and on the inner sides. Take one portion of the corn mixture and spread it on top of the potato base. Take a third portion of the potato and layer this on top of the corn. Spread the chutney on top of the potato. Take the second portion of the corn mixture and layer it on top. Finally place the last portion of the potatoes on top of the corn and seal the cake completely. Smooth the potato spread and place in a pre-heated oven at medium heat for approximately an hour. When pinkish in colour, remove from heat and allow it to cool for 10 minutes. Remove from the tin. Now spread the green pea paste all over the cake and smooth with a knife. Place on a serving dish and decorate as required.

1 tbsp. lemon juice
Grind together and make
chutney.

For the paste:
450 gm. (1 lb.) frozen green
peas
$1/2$ tsp. salt
1 tsp. butter

INGREDIENTS:
Part 1:
600 ml. (1 pint) of natural
yoghurt (sour if possible)
1 tbsp. gram flour
1 tbsp. chopped ginger and
chillies
1 tbsp. chopped coriander
leaves
1 tbsp. sugar
1 tsp. salt
$1/2$ tsp. turmeric powder
1 tsp. ground dhana-jeera
300 ml. ($1/2$ pint) water

Part 2 for the vaghaar:
1 tbsp. ghee or oil
$1/2$ tsp. mustard seeds
$1/2$ tsp. cumin seeds
$1/2$ tsp. coriander seeds
$1/2$ tsp. fenugreek seeds
Pinch of asafoetida
Few curry leaves
Few cloves and cinnamon
sticks

Part 3 for the Pakoras:
1 cup (8 oz.) wholemeal flour
$1/2$ tsp. salt
Pinch of bicarbonate of soda
1 boiled, mashed potato
2 tbsp. yoghurt
Water
Oil for frying

61: PAKODA KADHI

Mix all the ingredients for the pakoras and make a thick paste by adding water. Keep aside for 3-4 hours. Heat oil, make small balls out of the paste and fry them (like bhajis). Allow the pakoras to cool. Mix the gram flour, water and yoghurt and whisk together thoroughly. Add the remaining ingredients in Part 1 and boil together, stirring continuously for 10-15 minutes. Heat the ghee or oil in a frying pan (Part 2). Add the rest of the ingredients and when crackling pour over the boiling kadhi. When ready to serve, add the pakoras into the kadhi (Part 1). Boil for 3-5 minutes and serve hot.

Variations:
Half a cup of boiled peas and half a cup of boiled chopped potatoes can be added to the kadhi, with pakoras, to make a vegetable kadhi.
Serves 6-8.

INGREDIENTS:

For the paratha:
    1 cup (8 oz.) wholemeal flour
    1 tbsp. oil
    Water to make dough

For the stuffing:
    1 cup (8 oz.) mung dal
    1 tsp. garam masala
    1 tsp. sugar
    1 tsp. salt
    Juice of 1 lemon or 1/4 tsp. citric acid
    1 tbsp. chopped ginger and chillies

62: STUFFED MUNG DAL PARATHA

Mix the oil with the flour and make a soft dough by adding water, kneading thoroughly, and leave aside. Wash the dal thoroughly under running water and soak overnight. Drain the water from the dal, and cook in a saucepan. Add half a cup of water, cover the pan, reduce the heat and cook for 20-25 minutes, or until the water is absorbed and the dal is tender. Remove from heat, allow to cool and mash with hands. Add the rest of the ingredients for the stuffing and mix well. Divide the mixture into 4-5 portions. Divide the dough into 4-5 portions. Roll out each portion of dough into a circle of about 5 cm. in diameter. Place a portion of the stuffing in the centre of this, fold over the dough and press together firmly, then roll out again into a thick circle 10-12 cm. in diameter. Repeat with the rest of the dough and filling. Then cook as for paratha (Recipe No. 19).
Serves 4-5.

INGREDIENTS:

For the paste:
    4 tbsp. gram flour
    1/2 tsp. salt
    1/2 tsp. chilli powder
    1/4 tsp. turmeric powder

    Mix all these ingredients
    and water to make a paste.

    3 large capsicums cut into 4-5 pieces each

CAPSICUM KACHORI (A Variation on Moong Dal Paratha)

Place the moong dal stuffing inside the capsicum and press in well. Dip into the paste and deep fry.

INGREDIENTS:

    225 gm. (8 oz.) mava
    1 tbsp. ghee
    2 tbsp. icing sugar
    Chhanno made from 0.6 litres
    (1 pint) of full cream milk
    2 tbsp. of caster sugar
    1 tsp. cardamom powder
    2 tbsp. almond powder
    2 tbsp. pistachio powder
    2 tbsp. charoli
    1/2 tsp. ice-cream or vanilla essence

63: MAVA GHARI

Mash the chhanno thoroughly. Add the caster sugar and almond/pistachio powder and charoli. Grate the mava, add the ghee and heat on a low flame for about 5 minutes. Remove from heat and allow to cool. Add the icing sugar. Flatten the mava in the palm of your hand and place the milk stuffing in the centre of this. Roll up and tidy. Decorate with almonds, pistachios or sugar flowers.
4-5 pieces.

64: PANEER CURRY

INGREDIENTS:

Chhanno made from 2.4 litres
(4 pints) of full cream milk
225 gm. (8 oz.) liquidized
tomatoes
1/2 tsp. turmeric powder
1 tsp. salt or to taste
1 tsp. sugar
1 chopped onion
1 tbsp. oil
1/2 tsp. ghee
Ghee or oil to deep fry
chhanno (paneer)

For the paste:
4 tbsp. fresh or desiccated
coconut
1 piece of ginger
3 cloves of garlic
2 tbsp. poppy seeds
4 cloves
4 sticks of cinnamon
6 pieces of cardamom
10 chopped almonds
10 chopped cashew nuts
1 tbsp. chopped coriander
leaves
1 tsp. cumin seeds

Fry all the ingredients for the paste in 1 tablespoon of oil and grind together. Deep fry the chhanno (cut into small squares) and keep aside. Heat the oil and ghee and fry the onions for 1 minute. Add the tomatoes and boil for 5 minutes. Add the ground paste and chhanno and remaining ingredients and boil for a further 10 minutes. Serve hot.

Variation: Add boiled peas or sweetcorn to the gravy.
Serves 6-8.

65: CAULIFLOWER CURRY

INGREDIENTS:

1.8 kgs (4 lbs.) cauliflower
3/4 cup (6 oz.) fried cashew
nuts
2 cups (16 oz.) of strained
yoghurt (strain for at least 2
hours to remove all the
moisture)
1 tbsp. chopped ginger and
chillies
2 tbsp. chopped coriander
leaves
1 tsp. chilli powder
1 tbsp. dhana-jeera
1 tsp. garam masala
1/2 tsp. turmeric powder
4 tbsp. oil
1 tbsp. tomato ketchup
Oil to fry the cauliflower
Salt to taste

Cut the cauliflower into large pieces and place in a large pan of boiling water. Boil for 10 minutes. Remove from heat and drain off water completely using absorbent paper. Heat some oil in a deep frying pan and fry the cauliflower until pinkish in colour. Remove from heat, drain off excess oil and leave aside. Heat some oil in a frying pan and add the yoghurt and the remaining ingredients. Add half a cup of water and boil the gravy for a few minutes. Add cauliflower and boil for a further 10 minutes. (The curry should be quite thick.) Serve hot.
Serves 4-6.

INGREDIENTS:
- 3 cups (24 oz.) rice
- 2 tbsp. ghee
- 1 tbsp. oil
- 1/2 tsp. saffron
- 1 tbsp. butter
- 1/2 cup (4 oz.) milk
- 115 gm. (4 oz.) chopped french beans
- 115 gm. (4 oz.) chopped carrots
- 115 gm. (4 oz.) peas
- 115 gm. (4 oz.) chopped chori (green)
- 115 gm. (4 oz.) chopped potatoes
- Sugar, salt and lemon juice to taste
- 1 tbsp. chopped cashew nuts
- 1 tbsp. chopped raisins
- 1 tbsp. almonds and pistachios
- 1 tbsp. chopped dried apricots
- 1 tbsp. chopped ginger and chillies
- 1 tbsp. chopped kharek (dried dates)
- 1 tsp. garam masala
- 1 tin of pineapple pieces

66: BIRYANI

Heat the ghee and oil and fry all the vegetables (beans, carrots, peas, potatoes) and cook on a low flame until tender. Add the dried fruit, ginger and chillies, and remaining ingredients and garam masala. Drain pineapple and add to the mixture. Divide the cooked mixture into 2 equal parts and leave aside. Cook the rice as normal. Add salt and saffron and divide into 3 equal portions. Grease an ovenproof dish and layer it with one portion of the rice. Cover this with one portion of the vegetable mixture. Repeat with rice and rest of mixture. Top up with the last portion of rice. Add the milk. Dot with butter, cover with foil and cook in a pre-heated oven at medium temperature for 15-20 minutes. Serve hot. Serves 8-10.

INGREDIENTS:

Part 1:
- 900 gm. (2 lb.) grated carrots
- 600 ml. (1 pint) milk
- 1 cup (8 oz.) sugar
- 1 large carton double cream
- 1 tsp. ground cardamom
- 1 tsp. ground saffron
- 1 tbsp. chopped almonds
- 1 tbsp. chopped pistachio
- 2 tbsp. milk powder

Part 2:
- 1.8 kg. (4 lb.) white pumpkin, peeled and grated
- 4 cups milk
- 3 cups (24 oz.) sugar
- 4 tbsp. ghee
- 4 tbsp. milk powder
- 1/2 tsp. ground cardamom
- 1/2 tsp. ground saffron

67: ANNIVERSARY CAKE
(WHITE PUMPKIN AND CARROT CAKE)

Part 1:
Boil the carrots in the milk until the milk is fully absorbed. Add cream and sugar and stir slowly until the mixture becomes smooth and does not stick to the sides of the pan. Add milk powder and cardamom, saffron, almonds and pistachio. Stir well. Cool and leave aside. Refrigerate for 2 days if possible.

Part 2:
Repeat the above procedure with the pumpkin. Cool and leave aside. Refrigerate for 2 days if possible.

Take a 27 cm. square cake tin. Place the carrot mixture at the bottom of the tin and press down firmly. Place the pumpkin mixture on top of this, and press down well. Refrigerate for at least an hour. Remove from cake tin and decorate as required.

- 1 tbsp. ground almonds
- 1 tbsp. ground pistachio
- 1 large carton double cream

INGREDIENTS:
2 cups (8 oz.) rice
2 tbsp. oil
1 tbsp. ghee
5 small potatoes
3-4 small aubergines
5 small pickled onions
2 long carrots
25 gm. (1 oz.) coconut cream
6 tindoras
6 cloves
6 sticks of cinnamon
1 tsp. cumin seeds
Salt to taste

Masala for stuffing:
1 dessertspoon chopped ginger and chillies
1 dessertspoon coriander leaves
1 tbsp. grated coconut
1 tbsp. gram flour
1 tbsp. ground peanuts
1 tbsp. sesame seeds
1 tsp. chilli powder
1 tsp. turmeric powder
1 tsp. salt
2 tsp. sugar or to taste
Juice of 1 lemon

68: STUFFED RICE

Mix all the ingredients for the masala together. Wash and soak the rice for 15-20 minutes. Prepare all the vegetables according to type. Cut the carrots into 1 inch thin strips. Cut out the centres of all the vegetables and stuff the masala inside the scored vegetables. Heat the ghee and oil in a saucepan, add the cloves, cinnamon, and cumin seeds. Then fry the prepared vegetables. Drain the rice and add this to the vegetables. Mix the coconut cream in 3 cups of water and cook on a low flame. Keep the pan covered until the rice and vegetables are tender and water is fully absorbed. If required add more hot water. Serve hot.
Serves 6-8.

Pinch of asafoetida
1 tbsp. oil

INGREDIENTS:
1 cup (8 oz.) peas
1 cup (8 oz.) trimmed valor
4 tbsp. oil
4 cups water
Pinch of bicarbonate of soda
1 tsp. salt
2 tbsp. chopped coriander leaves
1 tbsp. chopped ginger and chillies
1 dessertspoon dhana jeera powder

For the koftas:
3/4 cup (6 oz.) chopped fenugreek leaves
1/2 cup (4 oz.) wholemeal flour
1/2 cup (4 oz.) gram flour
1 tsp. salt

69: GREEN KOFTA CURRY

Mix all the ingredients for the koftas, add a little water and make into a soft dough. Roll into very small oval balls. Keep aside. Mix the water and oil together and boil. Add a pinch of bicarbonate of soda, peas, valor and salt and boil for 2-3 minutes. Add the koftas and let the mixture cook on a low heat for a few minutes. When cooked (tender to touch) add the remaining ingredients. If the gravy is too thick add a little water. The curry should be quite thin. Serve hot.
Serves 4-5.

1 tbsp. chopped ginger and chillies
2 tbsp. oil
Pinch of asafoetida

INGREDIENTS:

450 gm. (1 lb.) kund
2 tbsp. arrowroot powder
1/2 tsp. lemon juice
Salt to taste
Oil to fry patties

For the stuffing:

3 cups (24 oz.) natural yoghurt (fresh)
1 tsp. ginger and chillies
1 tbsp. chopped coriander
leaves
1 tsp. sugar
1 tbsp. peanut powder
1 tsp. cumin seeds
Pinch of asafoetida
1/2 tsp. salt

70: KUND PATTIES

To make the stuffing: Drain the yoghurt by allowing it to strain in a muslin cloth for at least 4 hours. Then mix the stuffing ingredients together and leave aside.

Peel and steam the kund. When cooked mash thoroughly, add arrowroot powder, salt and lemon juice. Take a portion of the mashed kund and form a flat round using the palm of the hand. Place a ball of stuffing in the centre of this. Roll over and pat into a patty shape. Repeat until all the kund and stuffing is used up. Deep fry in oil until pinkish in colour. Serve hot.
Serves 6-8.

INGREDIENTS:

450 gm. (1 lb.) boiled small
potatoes (peeled)
6 tbsp. oil

For the sauce:

225 gm. (8 oz.) boiled or
frozen corn liquidized with
one cup of water
225 gm. (8 oz.) liquidized
tomatoes
2 tbsp. roasted ground peanuts
2 tbsp. grated coconut
1 tbsp. chopped ginger and
chillies
1 tbsp. chopped coriander
1 tbsp. chopped cashew nuts
1 tbsp. cornflour dissolved in
2 tbsp. of water
Salt, sugar and lemon juice to
taste

71: POTATO CURRY IN CORN SAUCE

Mix all the ingredients for the sauce together and boil for 5-7 minutes. Keep aside. Fry the potatoes in oil. Add salt. Let the potatoes fry for 5-7 minutes until cooked. Add the sauce and boil for 7-10 minutes. Serve hot.
Serves 4-5.

INGREDIENTS:

450 gm. (1 lb.) desiccated coconut
1 large carton double cream
225 gm. (8 oz.) icing sugar
1/4 tsp. ground cardamom
1 round cake tin or mould
450 gm. (1 lb.) mava
225 gm. (8 oz.) sugar
1 cup water
1 tbsp. ghee

72: SWEET FLOWER BASKET (COCONUT CAKE)

Mix coconut, cream and sugar and heat on a low flame until thoroughly mixed. When the mixture is smooth and does not stick to the sides of the pan add cardamom, mix and remove from heat. Grease the mould and place the coconut mixture in it. After 15 minutes, place the sweet on a dish and gently remove the mould. Place in refrigerator for 2 hours. Grate mava and heat it with the ghee for 5 minutes on a very low flame. Keep aside. Mix the sugar in 1 cup of water and make two taar syrup. Add the mava to the syrup and mix thoroughly until the mixture becomes smooth and does not stick to the sides of the pan. Remove from heat and allow to cool. Once cool, use a polythene sheet as a base to roll out the mava into a round shape, approximately 2 cm. thick. Place this on top of the coconut sweet, covering it completely. Seal off all the edges and smooth it down. Decorate as required.
Serves 8-10.

INGREDIENTS:

1 cup (8 oz.) black whole urad

1/3 cup kidney beans
1/2 cup (4 oz.) natural yoghurt
— whisked well
1 tbsp. chopped ginger and chillies
1 tbsp. coriander leaves
1 chopped onion
4 tomatoes
2 tsp. salt or to taste
1 tsp. chilli powder
1 tsp. garam masala
1 tsp. turmeric powder
1 tsp. dhana-jeera
1 tsp. lemon juice
1/3 cup (4 oz.) single cream
3 tbsp. ghee
2-3 curry leaves
1/4 tsp. mustard seeds
1/4 tsp. cumin seeds
1/4 tsp. asafoetida

73: MOGHALAI DAL

Soak the urad and kidney beans in plenty of water overnight. Cook in a pressure cooker until tender. Heat the ghee and add the mustard seeds, cumin seeds and asafoetida. When crackling, add the onions and tomatoes. Allow to cook for 2-3 minutes, stirring frequently. Add the rest of the ingredients except the cream and lemon juice and mix well. Allow the dal to boil. Simmer for 10-15 minutes stirring frequently. Finally, add the cream and lemon juice, stir and serve hot.
Serves 6-8.

INGREDIENTS:

1) For the rice:
    450 gm. (1 lb.) long grain rice
    1 cake tin or ring serving plate
    Salt, sugar to taste

2) For the orange portion:
    4 liquidized strained tomatoes
    1 tbsp. tomato ketchup
    2 grated carrots
    1 tbsp. butter or ghee
    1/2 tsp. salt
    1/2 tsp. sugar

3) For the white portion:
    115 gm. (4 oz.) boiled strained
    corn (frozen will do)

4) For the green portion:
    115 gm. (4 oz.) boiled, drained
    peas, keep aside
    1 tbsp. ghee or butter
    1/2 bunch fresh coriander
    leaves
    1 green capsicum
    1/2 tbsp. lemon juice
    1 tsp. sugar
    1/2 tsp. salt
    Mix these ingredients and
    liquidize to a paste (except
    peas).

74: THREE IN ONE RICE

Cook the rice as normal, adding salt to taste. Drain and cool. The rice grains should be separate.

To make the orange portion:
Melt the ghee in a saucepan, add the carrots and fry for 1 minute. Then add the remainder of the ingredients (in Part 2) and cook for 5 minutes. Stir in a third of the rice, mix well and keep aside.

To make the white portion:
Heat the ghee in a saucepan, add the corn, salt to taste, and stir in a third of the rice. Keep aside.

To make the green portion:
Heat the ghee in a saucepan, add the green paste and peas and cook for a minute. Add the remaining rice and stir well. Layer the three rice combinations in a greased ovenproof dish or a cake tin, cover with foil and bake in a pre-heated oven at medium heat for 10 minutes. When ready to serve, invert on to a serving plate. Serve hot. Decorate as required.
Serves 6-8.

INGREDIENTS:

For the coriander stuffing:
    1 cup (8 oz.) chopped coriander
    leaves
    2 tbsp. chopped ginger and
    chillies
    2 tbsp. chopped fresh mint
    leaves
    1 tsp. salt
    1 tsp. cumin seeds
    1 tsp. oil
    1 tbsp. ground peanuts
    1 tbsp. butter

75: CORIANDER PARATHA

Make paratha dough as in Recipe No. 30. Grind together all the ingredients to make a green chutney paste. Roll out the paratha as normal. Brush the inside with the green paste. Roll up like a Swiss roll. Roll out again into a paratha 10-15 cm. in diameter and cook as normal.
Serves 5-6.

INGREDIENTS:

450 gm. (1 lb.) potatoes
1 cup coconut milk or 115 gm.
(4 oz.) creamed coconut
1 tbsp. boiled peanuts
1 tsp. tamarind mixed with $1/2$
cup of water to make juice
1 tbsp. brown sugar
1 tbsp. desiccated coconut
1 tbsp. each of roasted ground
peanuts and sesame seeds
1 tbsp. chopped coriander
leaves
1 tsp. salt or to taste
$1/2$ tsp. chilli powder
1 tbsp. each of chopped
capsicum, celery and green
fennel
2 tbsp. oil
$1/2$ tsp. each of mustard seeds
and cumin seeds
Pinch of asafoetida

76: POTATOES IN COCONUT MILK

Boil the potatoes and cut into medium-sized cubes. Heat the oil and add the cumin and coriander seeds, asafoetida, peanuts and sesame seeds. Add the remaining ingredients (except potatoes) and heat on a high flame for 5 minutes, stirring continuously. Add the potatoes and 1 cup of water. Boil for 10-15 minutes. Serve hot. Serves 6-8.

INGREDIENTS:

6 capsicums, washed and cut
into 4 pieces each
1 cup (8 oz.) gram flour and
some water
1 tsp. salt
$1/2$ tsp. turmeric powder
Oil for frying

For the stuffing:
450 gm. (1 lb.) frozen corn
1 tbsp. ground peanuts
1 tbsp. chopped cashew nuts,
almonds, and dried apricots
1 tbsp. ginger and chillies
1 tbsp. coriander leaves
(chopped)
1 tsp. sugar
Salt to taste
Juice of $1/2$ lemon
1 tbsp. cornflour
$1/4$ cup of water

77: CAPSICUM BHAJIA

Boil the corn and mash it. Add cornflour and remaining ingredients for the stuffing. Keep on a low heat for 7-10 minutes, stirring continuously. Remove from heat and allow to cool. Mix the gram flour and water to make a paste (like a pancake). Add salt and turmeric powder. Stuff capsicum with the corn mixture (and press down well). Repeat until all the capsicum and corn has been used up. Heat the oil in a deep frying pan. Dip the stuffed capsicum in the gram flour paste and deep fry until pinkish in colour.
Serves 6-8.

INGREDIENTS:

450 gm. (1 lb.) shelled peas
225 gm. (8 oz.) mange-tout
1 tbsp. ginger and chillies
1 tsp. dhana-jeera
1 tbsp. salt or to taste
1 tbsp. chopped coriander
4 tbsp. oil
3 cups water
Pinch of bicarbonate of soda

For the kofta:

1 cup (8 oz.) finely-chopped fenugreek leaves (methi)
3/4 cup (6 oz.) wholemeal flour
2 tbsp. gram flour
1 tsp. salt
1 tbsp. chopped ginger and chillies
1/4 tsp. bicarbonate of soda
2 tbsp. oil

78: MANGE-TOUT AND KOFTA CURRY

To make the kofta:
Mix the flour and oil. Then mix the remaining ingredients. Make into a dough using water. Divide the mixture into small oval balls and keep aside.
Heat the oil and water and add soda. Add the peas and mange-tout. Let it boil on a low heat. Add the salt, ginger and chillies, coriander, and dhana-jeera. When the peas and mange-tout are nearly cooked, gently add the koftas one by one. Allow to boil at a low heat. When cooked completely remove from heat.
Serves 6-8.

INGREDIENTS:

1 cup (8 oz.) chhanno
2 cups (16 oz.) milk powder
1 cup (8 oz.) sugar
1 tbsp. ghee
1/2 tsp. ground cardamom seeds
1/2 cup water

For the stuffing:

170 gm. (6 oz.) mava
2 tbsp. desiccated coconut
2 tbsp. ghee
1 tsp. ground fennel seeds
2 tbsp. ground almonds and pistachios
115 gm. (4 oz.) caster sugar
1 tsp. ground cardamom
1/2 tsp. nutmeg powder
1 tsp. poppy seeds

79: MILK GHAARI

Boil the sugar in half a cup of water and make two taar syrup. Mash the chhanno and place in the syrup. Heat on medium heat for 5 minutes, stirring constantly. Mix some ghee in the milk powder and add to the syrup. Stir and remove from heat. Allow it to cool. Divide into 8 parts.

To make the stuffing:

Heat the ghee and fry the mava for 5 minutes on medium heat. Remove from the heat and add all the ingredients. Mix well and keep aside to cool. Divide into 8 parts. Take a little ghee in the palm of your hand and place the milk ball on it. Flatten into the shape of a patty. Place the stuffing ball in the centre of this and roll up. Flatten slightly again and decorate as required.
Serves 8.

INGREDIENTS:

A) Channa:
> **225 gm. (8 oz.) coarse chick peas (white)**
> **3 tomatoes**
> **Chillies and root ginger to taste**
> **1 onion**
> **4 cloves garlic**
> **1/2 tsp. turmeric powder**
> **2 tbsp. oil**
> **1/2 tsp. chilli powder**
> **1 dessertspoon chana masala**
> **3-4 cups water**
> **Coriander leaves and onion slices for garnishing**
> **Salt and lemon juice to taste**

Chana Masala:
> **1 tsp. coriander seeds**
> **1/2 tsp. cumin**
> **1 tsp. chilli powder**
> **1 tsp. mango powder**
> **1 tsp. pomegranate seeds**
> **6 cloves, peppercorns, cinnamon sticks**
> **A few bay leaves**
> **Grind these into a powder**
> **Keep the extra Masala in an airtight bottle**

B) Bhatura:
> **1 cup (8 oz.) self-raising flour**
> **1 tsp. salt**
> **1 tbsp. natural yoghurt**
> **1 tbsp. oil**
> **Lukewarm water**
> **Oil for frying**

80: CHANNA BHATURA

A) Channa:

Soak the chick peas overnight. Drain and cook in pressure cooker with water for 30 minutes, until tender. Remove the channa when cooled. Grind the tomatoes, garlic, chillies and ginger into a paste. Place two tablespoons of oil in a saucepan and fry paste for 5 minutes. Add channa masala, turmeric powder, chilli powder, sugar, salt and lemon. Then add the cooked chick peas (channa) and add to the mixture. Boil for 15 minutes. Garnish with coriander leaves and onion. Serve hot with bhatura.

B) Bhatura:

Mix the oil and salt into the flour and rub together gently. Add yoghurt and water and make a soft dough. Cover and keep at room temperature for 6-7 hours. Divide the dough into 6-8 parts and roll them into flat circular shapes of 10 cm. in diameter. Heat the oil in a deep frying pan. Fry the bhatura very lightly until they are puffed up, then turn over to brown the other side. Drain oil from bhatura on absorbent paper and serve with channa.
Serves 4-6.

INGREDIENTS:
> **1 cup (8 oz.) rice**
> **4 tbsp. oil**
> **1 chopped onion**
> **6 cloves of garlic**
> **1 tbsp. chopped green and red chillies, mixed**
> **1/2 tsp. saffron**
> **1 tsp. salt**
> **2-3 cups water**

81: SPANISH RICE

Wash the rice under running water. Heat the oil and fry the onion, garlic and chillies. Add rice, water and salt and cook on a low heat. Add water if required. When cooked, gently add the saffron, mix and serve hot.
Serve 4-6.

INGREDIENTS:
1 cup (8 oz.) peas
450 gm. (1 lb.) small potatoes
225 gm. (8 oz.) mange-tout
1 tsp. ajma (bishop-weed seed)
4 tbsp. oil
Salt to taste

For the paste:
1 large stick of ginger
6-7 chillies
1 cup (8 oz.) chopped coriander leaves
6-7 cloves of garlic
1 cooking apple
1 tbsp. sesame seeds
1 tbsp. ground peanuts
1 tbsp. chopped mint leaves
1 tbsp. poppy seeds
1 medium-sized onion
Grind to a paste.

82: GREEN PEAS, POTATO AND MANGE-TOUT CURRY

Prepare the vegetables according to type and boil. Heat the oil, add the ajma and fry the paste. Then add the cooked vegetables and salt. Add 1 cup of water and boil for 15 minutes.

INGREDIENTS:
A) Ingredients:
340 gm. (12 oz.) mung dal
115 gm. (4 oz.) urad dal
1 tbsp. wheatflour
1 tbsp. cooking oil
Salt to taste

B) Ingredients:
For the stuffing
1 cup (8 oz.) grated coconut
1 tsp. ghee
1/2 tsp. salt or to taste
1/2 tsp. sugar
Chopped chillies and ginger to taste
1 tsp. lemon juice
1 tbsp. chopped mixed dried fruit and nuts (almonds, cashew nuts, raisins, dates, figs, apricots)
Cooking oil for frying

To make the yoghurt gravy:
600 ml. (1 pint) of whipped yoghurt
Make a chutney of:
A handful of stoned dates
2 tsp. tamarind
1/2 tsp. chilli powder
1/2 tsp. cumin powder
1 tsp. salt
Chopped coriander leaves

83: YOGHURT GHUGHARA

Soak the dals overnight, then grind into a paste without adding water. Heat a tablespoon of oil, add wheatflour and salt (from A) and mix well. Add to the ground dal. Take a piece of muslin cloth and soak in water. Squeeze out and spread flat on a chopping board. Place a small quantity of the dal paste on the cloth and flatten in the shape of the puri. Place the coconut mixture (from B) on half of this circle. Fold over by lifting the cloth and pressing down the other half of the puri on to the coconut mixture. Seal well and deep fry. Repeat until all the dal and coconut mixture is used up.

To make the stuffing: Heat ghee, add stuffing ingredients, stir well and keep aside.

To make the yoghurt gravy:
When ready to serve, dip the ghughara in hot water for 2 minutes. Remove, squeeze out water by pressing gently, and arrange in a dish. Add yoghurt, salt, cumin powder and chilli powder. Pour over the date chutney. Decorate with coriander leaves.
Serves 6-8.

INGREDIENTS:

900 gm. (2 lb.) potatoes
5-6 tbsp. oil
1 tbsp. cashew nuts — halved
1 tbsp. pistachios — halved
1 tbsp. almonds
1 tbsp. chopped dried fruits
1 tbsp. dried apple, kharek
1 tbsp. desiccated coconut
1 tsp. poppy seeds
1 tsp. raisins
$1/2$ tsp. pepper
1 tsp. cumin seeds
Salt, sugar and lemon juice to taste

84: POTATO AND NUT CURRY

Peel the potatoes and slice into long thin strips. Place the oil in a saucepan, heat, add cumin seeds and potatoes. Cook on a low heat. When cooked add the remaining ingredients, stir and remove from heat. Serve hot.
Serves 7-8.

INGREDIENTS:

225 gm. (8 oz.) dates
1 tbsp. ghee

Mava stuffing:
225 gm. (8 oz.) grated mava
1 tsp. ghee
115 gm. (4 oz.) caster sugar
1 tbsp. desiccated coconut
1 tsp. ground fennel
1 tsp. poppy seeds
$1/2$ tsp. ground cardamom
$1/4$ tsp. ground nutmeg
$1/4$ tsp. ground saffron

85: KHAJUR GHAARI (DATE SWEET)

Place the ghee in a saucepan and fry dates over a low flame until they do not stick to the sides of the pan. Remove from heat and keep aside to cool. Fry mava in ghee for 3 minutes, remove from heat and add all the remaining ingredients. Mix well and allow to cool. When cooled, divide the date mixture and the mava mixture into 12 equal portions each. Take a portion of the dates and using the palm of your hand, flatten into a small round, flat shape (10-15 cm. in diameter). Place a portion of mava mixture in the centre of this and roll up. Flatten slightly to shape. Repeat for remaining portions. Decorate with marzipan or icing sugar flowers, if required.
Serves 10-12.

INGREDIENTS:

½ cup (4 oz.) channa dal
½ cup (4 oz.) rajma (kidney beans)
¼ cup (2 oz.) whole urad dal (black)

For the paste:

1 piece ginger (approx 7 cm. long)
10 cloves of garlic
1 onion
225 gm. (8 oz.) tomatoes
½ cup (4 oz.) chopped coriander leaves
5-6 green chillies
Grind all ingredients together.

86: SHAHI DAL

Wash and soak the dals, (urad, kidney beans, etc.) overnight. Cook them in a pressure cooker with water as required. When cooked, whisk thoroughly using an egg beater. Heat the ghee in a saucepan, add bay leaves and curry leaves. When sizzling, add tomato paste. Cook for 5 minutes on medium heat, stirring occasionally. Add the rest of the seasoning ingredients. Add the cooked dal and let the mixture cook for at least 10-15 minutes. Add water if required. Serve hot.
Serves 4-6.

For dal seasoning:

1 tsp. turmeric powder
1 tsp. red chilli
1 tbsp. dhana-jeera
3 tbsp. ghee
Juice of 1 lemon
5 curry leaves
4-5 bay leaves
Salt to taste
½ tsp. each mustard and cummin seeds

INGREDIENTS:

½ cup (4 oz.) rava (coarse)
½ cup (4 oz.) gram flour (coarse)
1 cup (8 oz.) maize flour (coarse)
3 tbsp. oil
1 cup (8 oz.) sour yoghurt
1 cup hot water
1 tbsp. chopped ginger and chillies
1 tsp. salt
½ tsp. turmeric powder
½ tsp. bicarbonate of soda
Oil for greasing
Fruit salt

87: RAVA (SEMOLINA) AND CORN DHOKLAS

Mix the flours together with the oil. Add yoghurt to make a thickish paste. Add warm water to make the paste more spreadable if necessary. Add salt, turmeric, ginger and chillies, and bicarbonate of soda and mix thoroughly. Heat some water in a large vessel. Grease a thali and place inside making sure it is slightly raised so that the water does not rise and go inside. In the meantime, place 2-3 spoons of the dhokla mixture in a separate bowl. Add ¼ teaspoon of fruit salt and mix thoroughly. Spread this mixture evenly on the heated thali. Cover and cook on medium heat for 10 minutes. Remove from heat, cut out into diamond shapes and serve hot with chutney. Prepare all the dhoklas this way until the mixture is used up.
Serves 8-10.

INGREDIENTS:

900 gm. (2 lb.) frozen corn (boil and keep aside)
2 tbsp. cornflour dissolved in a little water
Oil for frying
1 tbsp. chopped celery
1 tbsp. chopped capsicum
1 tbsp. ginger and chillies
Breadcrumbs
Salt to taste

88: CORN ROLLS

Liquidize one pound of the corn. Mix all the ingredients together except the oil and the breadcrumbs and cook on a low heat until thickened. Divide into equal parts. Pat into sausage shapes. Dip into the breadcrumbs and deep fry. Serve with chutney.
Serves 8-10.

89: GREEN TOOVAR IN COCONUT MILK

Heat oil. Add mustard and coriander seeds, cinnamon, cloves and asafoetida. Add the liquidized tomatoes. Cook for a few minutes and then add the rest of the ingredients, apart from the toovar. Cook for 5 minutes, stirring occasionally. Add the toovar and water and let it boil for at least 15 minutes. Serve hot.
Serves 5-6.

INGREDIENTS:
450 gm. (1 lb.) toovar (boiled)
55 gm. (2 oz.) creamed coconut
4 liquidized tomatoes
2 tbsp. ground peanuts
1 tbsp. green ginger and chillies
2 tbsp. chopped coriander leaves
1 tbsp. ground khus-khus (poppy seeds)
2 tbsp. oil
1 tbsp. grated coconut
5 cloves
3-4 sticks of cinnamon.
1/2 tsp. mustard seeds
1/2 tsp. coriander seeds
Pinch of asafoetida
1/2 cup water
Sugar and salt to taste

90: CREAM BALL CURRY

1) Boil the potatoes, skin and mash them. Mix 2 dessertspoons of water in the cornflour and mix thoroughly to make a paste. Mix the butter, salt, mashed potatoes and cornflour paste. Heat the mixture on a low heat for 10 minutes. Put aside to cool.

2) For the stuffing:
Heat 2 tablespoons of oil, add all the ingredients and fry for approximately 10 minutes. Take 2 tablespoons of the potato mixture (1 above) and keep aside. Take the remaining mixture and roll out to a flat paste. Stuff the potatoes with the fried stuffing and cover to make balls. Deep fry the balls.

3) For the gravy:
Chop the tomatoes, liquidize and strain. Heat the ghee in a pan, add the tomatoes and the remaining ingredients (except the corn-flour) and mix well. Dissolve the cornflour in 1 cup of water and add this to the mixture. Boil for 10-15 minutes. Serve the balls in a bowl and pour hot gravy over them. Add a swirl of fresh cream on top to garnish if required. Alternatively decorate with rose petals.
Serves 6-8.

INGREDIENTS:
1) Ingredients:
450 gm. (1 lb.) potatoes
1 dessertspoon cornflour
Salt to taste
1 dessertspoon butter

2) For the stuffing:
115 gm. (4 oz.) peas
115 gm. (4 oz.) chopped french beans
115 gm. (4 oz.) grated carrot (Boil these vegetables together.)
1 dessertspoon chopped kharek
1 dessertspoon chopped almonds
1 dessertspoon chopped pistachio
1 dessertspoon chopped cashew nuts
1 dessertspoon chopped dried dates
1 dessertspoon chopped raisins
1/4 tsp. ground cloves and cinnamon (mixed)
Salt, sugar and lemon juice to taste
2 tbsp. cooking oil

3) For the gravy:
900 gm. (2 lb.) tomatoes
2 tbsp. mashed potato mixture (from 1 above)
2 tbsp. ghee
2 cups water
1 dessertspoon cornflour
1/2 tsp. turmeric powder
1 tsp. chilli powder
1 tbsp. each ground cashew nuts, almonds, pistachios
A few bay leaves and curry leaves
Salt and sugar to taste
1 tbsp. ground dhana-jeera
1 tsp. chopped mint leaves
1 dessertspoon ground ginger and chillies

INGREDIENTS:

250 gm. (9 oz.) mango pulp (tinned)
125 gm. (4^1/$_2$ oz.) sugar
125 gm. (4^1/$_2$ oz.) ground almonds
3 tbsp. milk powder
1 tbsp. ghee
1 round cake board 35 cm. in diameter
1 cup (8 oz.) desiccated coconut
4.8 litres (8 pints) milk
4 cups (32 oz.) icing sugar
2 cups (16 oz.) ground pistachios and almonds
1 tsp. cardamom powder
^{1}/$_2$ tsp. saffron
A few orange Smarties (or sweets)
A few chocolate drops
A chocolate butterfly
Some chocolate powder
A little green food colour

91: SUNFLOWER SWEET (MANGO AND ALMOND)

Mix the sugar in the mango pulp and boil the mixture. Add ground almonds and some ghee and cook on a low flame. Stir occasionally. When the mixture becomes paste-like and does not stick to the sides of the pan, add the milk powder, stir and remove from heat. Allow to cool. Make chhanno, add the icing sugar, ground pistachio and almonds, saffron and cardamom. Take a thali and grease it with a little ghee. Place the chhanno in the thali and boil in a double boiler for 7 minutes. Remove from heat and allow to cool. Place some clingfilm on the cake board. Place the chhanno on the board and spread it evenly all over. Roll the mango paste out into a thick round shape. place this on top of the chhanno. Using a knife, cut out the edges to resemble a sunflower. Colour the desiccated coconut green using the food colour. Decorate around the sunflower with this. Decorate with Smarties, chocolates and chocolate butterfly as shown.

INGREDIENTS:

1 cup (8 oz.) channa (gram) flour
450 gm. (1 lb.) mixed vegetables
(ladies fingers, guvaar, potatoes, aubergines)
225 gm. (8 oz.) tomatoes
2 tbsp. ginger and chillies
A few curry leaves and chopped coriander leaves

For the seasoning:
^{1}/$_2$ tsp. mustard seeds
^{1}/$_2$ tsp. cumin seeds
^{1}/$_2$ tsp. fenugreek seeds
Pinch of asafoetida
^{1}/$_2$ tsp. turmeric powder
6 sticks of cinnamon
6 cloves

1 tsp. salt
1 tsp. chilli powder
1 tsp. tamarind (soaked in ^{1}/$_2$ cup of water and ground to paste and strained)

92: SINDHI KADHI

Wash the vegetables and cut according to type. Cut the potatoes into long thin strips. Heat the ghee and oil in a large saucepan, add curry leaves and all the seasoning ingredients (except the salt, chilli and turmeric powder) and when sizzling add the gram flour. Fry the mixture on a low heat until the flour is pinkish in colour. Then add the salt, chilli and turmeric powder and 6 cups of water. Boil for a few minutes and add the prepared vegetables. Once these are cooked in the kadhi add the coriander, kokam, sugar, tomatoes, ginger, chillies and tamarind. Allow the mixture to boil for a few minutes. Serve hot.
Serves 8-10.

**A few kokams (soaked in $1/2$
cup of water)
Brown sugar to taste
3 tbsp. cooking oil
1 tbsp. ghee**

INGREDIENTS:

**2 cups (16 oz.) rice
225 gm. (8 oz.) frozen corn
$1/2$ tsp. cumin seeds
1 tbsp. ghee
$1/2$ tsp. salt**

**Making the chutney:
1 bunch of coriander leaves
1 tbsp. ground coconut
6 green chillies
1 tsp. sugar
1 tsp. salt
Juice of 1 lemon
Grind together to make a
paste**

93: CORN RICE

Cook the rice as normal. Place the corn in boiling water and cook for a few minutes. Heat the ghee in a saucepan, add the cumin seeds and salt. Add the corn and rice and stir together gently.

Variations: Chutney corn rice.
Cook as above and stir in chutney.

INGREDIENTS:

**1 medium-sized loaf of thinly-
sliced bread
Oil for deep frying**

**For the stuffing:
1 cup (8 oz.) boiled green peas
or frozen peas
3 medium-sized boiled
potatoes, cut into small
pieces
3 grated carrots
$1/2$ cup (4 oz.) shredded white
cabbage
1 chopped onion
$1/2$ cup (4 oz.) boiled channa
dal (soak the dal overnight,
boil until tender, drain and
cool)
1 tbsp. chopped ginger and
green chillies
1 tbsp. chopped coriander
leaves
1 tsp. garam masala
Salt, sugar and lemon to taste**

94: BREAD GHUGHARA

Mix all the following ingredients: vegetables, dal, onion, chillies, ginger, coriander, salt, sugar, lemon juice and masala. Mix well and keep aside. Cut the crusts of the bread. Spray a little water on to each slice, then roll out using a rolling pin. Cut using a round biscuit cutter and stuff with the previously prepared stuffing mixture. Shape like a ghughara (cylindrical) and press the edges in neatly. Deep fry in hot oil. Serve hot.
Serves 6-8.

INGREDIENTS:
450 gm. (1 lb.) French beans
Pinch of bicarbonate of soda
2 tbsp. of oil

For the masala:
2 tbsp. desiccated coconut (preferably fresh)
1 tbsp. khus-khus
1 tbsp. chopped ginger and chillies
2 tbsp. chopped coriander leaves
Grind to a paste.

1 tbsp. coconut fresh or desiccated
1 tbsp. chopped coriander leaves
Salt to taste

95: FRENCH BEAN CURRY (IN COCONUT MILK)

Prepare the beans and chop finely. Boil some water, add salt and bicarbonate of soda and add beans. Cook until tender. (Keep the pan uncovered while cooking, so the beans remain green.) Remove from heat and keep aside. Heat the oil in a pan and fry the masala paste for 5 minutes. Add the beans and salt to taste. Allow to cook on a medium heat for 5 minutes. Do not add water. Stir occasionally. Remove from heat and garnish with desiccated coconut and coriander leaves. Serve hot.
Serves 6-8.

INGREDIENTS:
450 gm. (1 lb.) baby potatoes
Oil to fry potatoes
A few toothpicks
1 tablespoon cornflour mixed in half a cup of water
Salt to taste

Masala for stuffing:
1/2 cup grated coconut, preferably fresh
1 tbsp. chopped almonds, pistachio, charoli (mixed)
1 tbsp. chopped dried dates, apricots, raisins
1 tbsp. chopped ginger chillies
1 tsp. red chilli powder
1 tbsp. chopped coriander leaves
1 tbsp. sugar
Juice of 1 lemon
Salt to taste
Mix all the masala and keep aside

96: ROYAL DAM ALOO

Boil the potatoes well in salted water. Remove from heat and place in cold water. Peel, and cut out the tops of the potatoes. (approximately 1/4). Scoop out potato flesh gently from the potatoes. Mix the scooped potato with the masala stuffing mixture. Place this back in the potatoes (as originally scooped out), replace the tops and keep in place using toothpicks. Heat the oil, and fry the potatoes (including the toothpicks) and keep aside. Heat 1 tablespoon of oil in a separate pan, and add the gravy masala (the ground portion only). Allow to cook for 5 minutes. Add the liquidized tomatoes. Add the tomato ketchup, sugar, salt and chilli powder. Add the pineapple juice and pomegranate seeds. Boil, and add the cornflower mixed in water. When boiling, add the fried potatoes. Boil for 10 minutes. If the curry looks too thick, add a little water. When serving, decorate with sprinkling mixture.
Serves 6 to 8.

For the gravy:
   1 tbsp. oil
   1 onion
   1 tsp. cumin powder
   1 tsp. coriander seeds
   1 tsp. poppy seeds
   6 peppercorns, 6 cinnamon sticks, 6 cloves

2 tbsp. dessicated coconut
2 tbsp. ground cashewnut
Grind these together and keep aside
1 cup fresh or tinned pineapple juice
1 lb liquidised tomatoes
1 tsp. chilli powder

Sugar and salt to taste
1 tbsp. tomato ketchup

For sprinkling on top:
   1 tbsp. chopped coriander leaves
   1 tbsp. dessicated coconut
   1 pomegranate — deseeded

INGREDIENTS:

   2 cups (16 oz.) rice
   225 gm. (8 oz.) frozen corn
   1/2 tsp. cumin seeds
   1 tbsp. ghee
   1/2 tsp. salt

97: CORN RICE:

Cook the rice making sure the grains remain separate and fluffy. Boil some water and add the corn. Cook for 5 minutes. Drain and keep aside. Heat the ghee in a pan, add the cumin seeds, rice, corn and salt. Mix gently, cook for a few minutes and remove from heat. Serve hot.

Variation: You can add freshly made green chutney to the rice, stir gently and serve as normal. (For chutney recipe see Appendix.)
Serves 6-8.

98: SWEET ASSORTMENT

1. Date samosas
2. Date rolls
3. Date snowballs
4. Coconut ghaari
5. Double decker
6. Fig barfi
7. Milk ghaari; carrots and

pumpkin halwa
8. Tricolour mango and nut sweet
9. Chocolate, almond and pistachio truffle
10. Mava ghaari
11. Pineapple sweet

Decorate these as required.

1/2/3. INGREDIENTS:

   250 gm (9 oz.) stoned dates
   1 tbsp. ghee

For the stuffing:
   2 tbsp. almond powder
   2 tbsp. pistachio powder
   2 tbsp. cashew nut powder
   2 tbsp. condensed milk
   1 tbsp. desiccated coconut
   1/2 tsp. saffron
   1/2 tsp. cardamom
   1/4 tsp. ground nutmeg
   1 tsp. ghee

1) Date Samosas:
Heat the ghee in a non-stick pan and add the dates. Cook on a low heat until no longer sticky, stirring constantly. Leave aside to cool. Mix the stuffing ingredients together. Divide the date mixture and the stuffing into three equal parts. Take the first part to make the samosas. This should make 4-5 samosas. Roll out some of the date mixture on to a pastry board covered with a piece of nylon cloth. The rolled-out mixture should be as thin as that for a chapatti. Divide into 2 semicircular shapes and fold into a cone shape (like a samosa). Put the stuffing in and seal the edges. Repeat until all this part of the date mixture is used up.

2) Date rolls:
Roll out the mixture into a large thick round. Spread the stuffing on top, patting evenly with your fingers. Then roll up like a Swiss roll. Wrap in aluminium foil and refrigerate. Before serving, remove from foil and slice.

Note: The recipe is the same for:
Date samosas
Date rolls
Date snowballs
This should make 20-25
pieces, depending on size

4) INGREDIENTS:
55 gm. (2 oz.) desiccated
coconut
4 tbsp. single cream
1/2 cup milk
4 tbsp. sugar

For the stuffing:
Chhanno made from 600 ml.
(1 pint) full cream milk
2 tbsp. condensed milk
2 tbsp. ground almonds
1 tsp. ghee
1/2 tsp. saffron
1/4 tsp. nutmeg

5) INGREDIENTS:
Chhanno made from 2.4 litres
(4 pints) full cream milk
2 tbsp. grated mava
3 tbsp. milk powder
3/4 cup (6 oz.) sugar
2 tbsp. ghee
2 tbsp. chocolate powder
2 tbsp. desiccated coconut
1 tbsp. ground cardamom

6) INGREDIENTS:
200 gm. (7 oz.) dried figs
1 cup milk
3 cups (24 oz.) grated mava
3/4 cup (6 oz.) sugar
3 tbsp. milk powder
1 tbsp. ghee

7) INGREDIENTS:
Chhanno made from 1.2 litres
(2 pints) full cream milk
1/2 cup (4 oz.) sugar
1 cup (8 oz.) milk powder

3) Date snowballs:
(You should get 4-6 of these.)
Roll out small flat rounds (approximately 7 cm. in diameter). Place the stuffing in the centre of each round and roll up into a ball. Dust the balls with desiccated coconut.

4) Coconut ghaari:
(You should get four pieces)
Heat the first group of ingredients over a low flame, stirring continuously. Cook until the mixture is well blended and does not stick to the sides of the pan. Remove from heat and keep aside. Heat the chhanno and condensed milk in a separate pan on a low flame. Cook until smooth and does not stick to the sides of the pan, then add the rest of stuffing ingredients. Remove from heat and put aside to cool. When both are cool, take the coconut portion and divide into 4 parts. Repeat for stuffing. Roll out the coconut into a small flat round with your hands. Place a ball of stuffing in the centre of this. Roll up and flatten, like a patty. Repeat using the rest of the mixture.

5) Double decker:
Heat the chhanno and sugar in a pan over a low flame and cook until thick and it does not stick to the sides of the pan. Mix the mava, milk powder and ghee and add to the chhanno. Add the desiccated coconut. Cook until ingredients are well mixed and do not stick to the pan. Remove from heat and divide into 2 portions. Mix the chocolate powder into one portion and cardamom into the other. Grease a large round thali or baking dish. Roll out the chocolate mixture. Repeat with the cardamom mixture and place this on top of the chocolate. Using a biscuit cutter, cut out rounds of the sweet. Decorate as required.

6) Fig Barfi:
(Makes 15-20 pieces, depending on size)
Soak the figs in the milk for 5-6 hours, then liquidize. Heat the mixture in a saucepan over a low heat. Add the sugar and cook until thick and it does not stick to the sides of the pan. Add the mava, milk powder and ghee. Cook again until thick and consistent. Allow to cool. Cut out into shapes using biscuit cutter or shape into leaf shapes.

7) Halwa Ghaari:
(You should get 4-5 pieces)
Mash the chhanno. Mix the sugar and water and heat in a saucepan to make two taar syrup. Add the chhanno and heat for 5-7 minutes. Add the ghee and milk powder (mixed thoroughly) and cook until

2 tsp. ghee
¹/₄ cup water

For the stuffing:
225 gm. (8 oz.) grated white pumpkin
1 cup milk
4 tbsp. sugar
4 tbsp. fresh double cream
¹/₂ tsp. cardamom
A few drops green food colour

For the stuffing:
225 gm. (8 oz.) grated carrot
1 cup milk
4 tbsp. sugar
4 tbsp. fresh double cream
¹/₂ tsp. cardamom

8) INGREDIENTS:
1 cup (8 oz.) ground cashew nuts
¹/₂ cup (4 oz.) tinned mango pulp
¹/₄ cup (2 oz.) sugar
1 tsp. ghee

For stuffing number one:
¹/₂ cup (4 oz.) shelled almonds (place in hot water and remove skin)
¹/₂ cup milk
2 tbsp. sugar

For stuffing number two:
¹/₂ cup (4 oz.) pistachio nuts (repeat as for almonds)
¹/₄ tsp. cardamom

9) INGREDIENTS:
1 slab plain chocolate (250 gm.)
The remainder as for the almond and pistachio sweet in the Tricolour Sweet.

11) INGREDIENTS:
Make the milk portion as in the Halwa Ghaari recipe.
1 tin pineapple pieces

it does not stick to the sides of the pan. Mix the ghee and milk powder. Keep aside.

For the white pumpkin halwa:
Heat the milk and the grated pumpkin on a low flame until the milk is fully absorbed. Then add the sugar and the double cream. When cream is fully absorbed, add the cardamom. Put aside to cool. Make the carrot halwa in the same way. When all three are cool, roll out the chhanno into a small round. Place some white pumpkin halwa on this. Place the carrot halwa on top. Roll up and flatten like a patty. Repeat until all the mixture is used up.

Decorate as required.

8) Tricolour mango and nut sweet:
(You should get 6-7 pieces)
Soak almonds in milk for 3-4 hours and grind to a paste. Heat the almond paste over a low flame. Add sugar and cook until thick and it does not stick to the sides of the pan, and add cardamom. Repeat for pistachio.

To make the shell of the sweet:
Heat the mango pulp and sugar. When boiled and thick, add cashew nut powder. Cook stirring constantly until it becomes a thick paste. Add the ghee to milk powder and mix thoroughly. Add this to the cooking mango and nut mixture and boil. Remove from heat and allow to cool. Divide all three sweets into 6-7 equal parts. Take part of the almond sweet and roll out into a small flat round. Add the pistachio sweet to this. Finally add the mango sweet and roll up into a large ball. Divide this ball (using a knife) into 4 equal parts. Repeat until all the sweets are used up.

9) Chocolate, almond and pistachio truffle:
Make the almond and pistachio sweets and roll out together into a ball. Heat the chocolate in a double boiler. Dip the sweet balls individually into the melted chocolate, covering completely, and remove. Repeat until all the sweet and chocolate is used up.

10) Mava Ghaari — as in Recipe no. 63

11) Pineapple sweet:
(You should get 4-5 pieces)
Drain the pineapple thoroughly on kitchen paper. Roll out the chhanno into small rounds. Place the pineapple in the centre and roll up into a patty shape. Repeat until all the mixture is used up.

99: INDIAN WEDDING PARTY SWEETS

1. Sweet Sari (Mango cake recipe number 54)
2. Sweet Turban (Semolina Cake)
3. Carrot Ghaari
4. Sweet Strawberry Samosas

1) INGREDIENTS:

For the decoration:
    1 cardboard box (like a shirt box)
    Red paper to cover the box
    1/4 packet marzipan
    Silver cake decorations (balls)

2) INGREDIENTS:
    1 cup (8 oz.) semolina
    1 cup (8 oz.) gram flour
    1 tbsp. ghee
    1 tbsp. milk
    2 cups (16 oz.) desiccated coconut
    1 cup (8 oz.) ghee and 1 cup (8 oz.) powdered almonds
    1 cup (8 oz.) sugar
    1 cup water
    1 tsp. cardamom
    1/2 tsp. saffron
    1/2 tsp. nutmeg
    2 cups grated mava

For the decoration:
    3 cups (24 oz.) powdered almonds
    1 cup (8 oz.) sugar
    1/2 cup water
    A piece of nylon (to roll out the pastry on)

3) INGREDIENTS:
    1 cup (8 oz.) grated carrots, cooked in steam
    2 cups (16 oz.) mava
    1/2 cup (4 oz.) icing sugar
    1 tbsp. ghee

For the shell:
    1/2 cup (4 oz.) powdered almonds

1) Sweet sari:
Make the mango cake as per recipe number 54. Divide the marzipan into three portions. Colour these blue, green and red respectively. Make flowers out of the blue and red marzipan, as shown in the photograph. Colour in, using the green marzipan and the silver balls. Cover the box with red paper, and place the mango sweet in the box. (This should be done before the sweet is decorated.) Make the box shallow by placing another piece of card as a 'false bottom'.

2) Sweet turban:
Heat 1 tablespoon of milk and 1 tablespoon of ghee and mix this into the gram flour. Keep aside. Heat 1 cup of ghee in another saucepan, and add the semolina. Roast this for ten minutes, stirring all the time and then add the prepared gram flour. Roast this mixture on a low heat for 25 minutes. Add the mava, coconut and almonds — mix well and remove from heat. Add the cardamom, saffron and nutmeg. Make a syrup with one cup of water and 1 cup of sugar (one taar). Remove from heat and add the above mixture to the syrup. Place the sweet in a round mould or vessel to set for a few hours. When ready to decorate, turn out on to a cake dish or plate.

For the decoration:
Boil the water and then add the sugar and boil for a further 5 minutes. Add the almonds and cook stirring continuously until the mixture is smooth and it does not stick to the sides of the pan. Remove from heat and allow to cool. Using a rolling pin and the nylon cloth (as a base), roll out the prepared pastry. Cover the round sweet prepared earlier with this. With the remaining pastry, cut out strips and place on top of the sweet, to look like the pleats of the turban, as in the picture. Decorate with red and silver balls (cake decorations).

3) Carrot ghaari:
Heat the ghee, and add the carrots and mava. Cook for a while, then remove from heat, add the sugar and keep aside to cool.

For the shell:
Heat the ghee, add the almonds and pistachio and allow to cook over a low flame for 5 minutes. Add the milk powder, mix and remove from heat. Mix the water and sugar to make two taar syrup, and add the roasted almond and pistachio mixture to the syrup. Add the saffron and cardamom, mix and remove from heat. Divide

$^1/_2$ **cup (4 oz.) powdered**
pistachios
1 cup (8 oz.) milk powder
$^1/_2$ **cup (4 oz.) sugar**
$^1/_4$ **cup water**
1 tbsp. ghee
$^1/_2$ **tsp. saffron**
1 tsp. ground cardamom

4) INGREDIENTS:
450 gm. (1 lb.) strawberries
3 cups (24 oz.) cashew nuts
$^1/_4$ **cup water**
1 cup (8 oz.) sugar
Stuffing as required e.g.
mango stuffing

INGREDIENTS:
2 carrots, finely grated
2 cucumbers, finely grated
100 gms. finely chopped
cabbage
1 small tin of pineapple
cubes

FOR THE DRESSING:
1 tablespoon vinegar
1 tablespoon salad oil
$^1/_2$ **teaspoon salt**
$^1/_4$ **teaspoon pepper**
1 teaspoon sugar
$^1/_4$ **teaspoon mustard paste**
Mix the dressing thoroughly
in a shaker or tightly capped
bottle.

FOR THE TOPPING:
8 ozs curd cheese
4 tablespoons natural yoghurt

into 10-12 parts and roll each part into a ball. Take the carrot-mava mixture and divide into 10-12 parts. Take one part into the palm of your hand, place the almond-pistachio ball in the centre and roll up and shape as in the photograph. Decorate as required.

4) Strawberry samosas and ghugharas:
Wash the strawberries and liquidize. Strain to extract one cup of juice. Boil the strawberry juice, water and sugar for 5 minutes. Reduce the heat and add the cashew nuts and cook until the mixture is smooth and does not stick. Remove from heat and allow to cool.

For the ghugharas:
Using a nylon cloth as a base, roll out the strawberry paste and stuff with any stuffing (I have used the mango stuffing as in the mango cake — recipe number 54). Then shape into ghughara.

For the samosa:
As for the ghughara, but roll up into the shape of a samosa.

100: EXOTIC SALAD

Take half the dressing and put the other half aside. Mix some of it onto the grated carrot.
Repeat with the cucumber, and the cabbage, but keep all three separate. Squeeze out excess moisture from all the grated vegetables. Place the cucumber on the bottom of a loaf tin. Mix the pineapple cubes onto the cabbage, ensure all moisture is drained off, and place this cabbage mixture on top of the cucumber. Finally, place the carrots on top. Refrigerate for an hour or so.
Mix the curd cheese, yoghurt and the remaining half of the dressing, thoroughly.
Unmould the salad onto a serving plate. Cover, with the curd cheese topping, and press down using a flat knife. Refrigerate again for a while. Decorate as required.

INGREDIENTS:

2 cups chhanno
3/4 cup icing sugar
1/2 teaspoon icecream essence
(or banana essence)
1 cup ground pistachio nuts
2 tablespoons milk powder
1/2 cup sugar
1/2 teaspoon ghee

101: PISTACHIO SANDESH

Finely mash the chhanno, add the icing sugar and essence and mix thoroughly. Make two taar syrup with the sugar, Remove from heat, and add the pistachio and milk powder.

Divide the chhanno into two parts. Grease a spread and place one part of the channo on it. Spread the pistachio mixture on top of this. Finally spread the remaining half of the channo on top of the pistachio spread. Allow to set for a while. Using a biscuit cutter, cut out shapes. Decorate as required.

Note: You can add green food colour to the pistachio paste for a brighter effect.

INGREDIENTS:

3/4 cup condensed milk
2 cups grated coconut
1/2 teaspoon cardamon powder
1/2 teaspoon saffron
2 cups chhanno
3/4 teaspoon ghee

102: COCONUT SANDESH

Finely mash the channo and mix the icing sugar, Cook over a low heat, stirring frequently, for five to ten minutes. If it feels too soft then cook and stir for some more time.

Mix the coconut, condensed milk, saffron, and cardamon and cook over a medium heat for five minutes.

Grease a thali with the ghee, and then spread the chhanno on it. Spread the coconut mixture on top. Allow to set for a while. Then cut using a biscuit cutter and decorate as required.

SALADS AND DRESSINGS:

INGREDIENTS:

1 1/2 cups (12 oz.) yoghurt (drained well)
1/2 tsp. mustard powder or paste
1 tsp. lemon juice
Salt to taste
1/2 tsp. pepper
2 tbsp. oil
1 tbsp. finely chopped mint leaves (optional)

1) Yoghurt 'Mayonnaise':

Mix all the ingredients and stir well using a wooden spoon. Place in an airtight container and chill.

INGREDIENTS:

1 ripe avocado
1 tbsp. lemon juice
2/3 cup yoghurt (drained well)
1/2 tsp. tabasco sauce
Salt to taste
1 tbsp. mayonnaise (optional)

2) Avocado Dressing:

Scoop out all the flesh from the avocado and liquidize with the remaining ingredients. Use immediately. This can be used as a dip with vegetable crudites (carrots, capsicum, celery, etc. cut into long strips). It can also be used as a 'chutney'. Alternatively serve with cocktail snacks.

INGREDIENTS:
1 cup (8 oz.) yoghurt (drained well)
2 tbsp. finely chopped parsley
2 tbsp. finely chopped spring onions
1 tbsp. finely chopped fresh fennel
Salt to taste
$1/2$ tsp. black pepper
1 tbsp. oil

3) Herb Yoghurt Dressing:
Mix all the ingredients thoroughly. Place in an airtight container and chill. Use with any fresh salad.

INGREDIENTS:
1 cup (8 oz.) yoghurt
1 tbsp. finely chopped coriander leaves
1 tbsp. finely chopped capsicum (any colour)
1 tbsp. finely chopped fresh fennel
1 tbsp. finely chopped mint leaves (optional)
$1/2$ tsp. chilli powder
Salt to taste
1 tbsp. sweetcorn relish

4) Herb Yoghurt Dressing — 2:
Thoroughly mix all the ingredients. Place in an airtight container and chill. Use in any kind of salad.

INGREDIENTS:
1 cup (8 oz.) yoghurt (drained well)
1 tbsp. finely chopped chives
1 tbsp. finely chopped capsicum (or ground)
$1/2$ tsp. pepper
1 tbsp. oil
1 tbsp. chopped walnuts
1 tbsp. tomato ketchup
Salt to taste

5) Herb Yoghurt Dressing — 3:
Mix all the ingredients thoroughly. Place in an airtight container and chill. This dressing can be used in all salads.

INGREDIENTS:
450 gm. (1 lb.) shredded white cabbage
2 grated carrots
1 grated apple
1 grated beetroot — small (optional)
1 small onion, grated (optional)
3 tbsp. chopped walnuts
1 cup (8 oz.) yoghurt mayonnaise

6) Coleslaw:
Mix all the ingredients in a large bowl and mix thoroughly. Chill for 2 hours. Serve cold.

INGREDIENTS:

900 gm. (2 lb.) boiled potatoes
(cut into pieces)
1 finely chopped onion
2 tbsp. olive oil (or salad oil)
1 tbsp. white vinegar
1/2 tsp. salt
1 1/2 cup (12 oz.) yoghurt
mayonnaise
1 tbsp. chopped fresh chives
(or parsley or coriander)

7) Potato Salad:

Cool the potatoes. Mix the vinegar, oil and salt. Then pour the yoghurt mayonnaise on to the potatoes. Mix well and chill. Before serving garnish with chives, parsley or coriander.

INGREDIENTS:

1 cup (8 oz.) cooked red kidney beans
1 cup (8 oz.) cooked haricot beans
1 cup (8 oz.) any other kind of cooked beans
Cool these
1 small finely chopped onion
2 tbsp. finely chopped parsley
1 cup (8 oz.) yoghurt mayonnaise
Salt and pepper to taste

8) Bean Salad:

Mix all the ingredients in a bowl and allow to cool at room temperature.

INGREDIENTS:

1 thinly sliced pear
1 thinly sliced apple
Toss these in a little lemon juice
1 1/2 cups (12 oz.) finely shredded cabbage
1 carrot cut into thin strips
4 dried figs finely chopped
2 tsp. sesame seeds
1/4 cup (2 oz.) yoghurt mayonnaise
1/4 cup (2 oz.) sour cream
1 tbsp. sunflower seeds
Salt to taste

9) Fruit and Seed Coleslaw:

Toss the sunflower seeds in a dry saucepan over heat until golden brown. Cool. Mix the sunflower seeds, sesame seeds, chopped figs, mayonnaise and cream. Chill. When ready to serve mix with the remaining ingredients and serve.

INGREDIENTS:

1 1/2 cups (12 oz.) boiled pasta
1/2 cup (4 oz.) sour cream
4 tbsp. natural yoghurt
1 clove crushed garlic
1 tbsp. tabasco sauce
1 tbsp. chopped parsley

10) Pasta Salad:

Mix the cream, yoghurt, tabasco sauce, garlic and parsley. Add the salt and pepper and chill. Mix pasta, asparagus, pine nuts and the dressing. Store at room temperature before serving.

**115 gm. (4 oz.) asparagus tips
(boiled in salted water)
1 tbsp. toasted pine nuts
Salt and pepper to taste**

INGREDIENTS:

**For the salad dressing:
2 tbsp. chopped roasted
peanuts
2 tbsp. peanut oil
1 tsp. soya sauce
1 tsp. chilli sauce
1 tbsp. smooth peanut butter
1 tbsp. lemon juice
Salt to taste**

11) Peanut Salad:
Mix all the ingredients and chill before use with other salads.

**A sample salad:
1 cup (8 oz.) beetroot
1 red pepper cut into thin
slices
2-3 sticks of celery
1 cup (8 oz.) shredded cabbage**

INGREDIENTS:

**1 avocado thinly sliced (add
lemon juice to prevent
discolouring)
2 peeled oranges
1 tbsp. finely chopped parsley
For the dressing:
1 tsp. vinegar
1 tsp. oil
1 tsp. sugar
1/2 tsp. mustard paste
1/2 tsp. pepper
1/2 tsp. salt**

12) Avocado Salad:
Mix the avocado, oranges and finely chopped parsley and put aside. Place the ingredients for the dressing in a screw top jar and shake thoroughly. Pour over the avocado and orange segments, mix well and serve.
Variation: Mix spring onions and tomatoes into the dressing, or add chopped flat parsley.

INGREDIENTS:

**1/2 cup (4 oz.) cracked wheat
1 bunch of finely chopped
spring onions
2 chopped tomatoes**

13) Cracked Wheat Salad:
Soak cracked wheat for at least half an hour and boil for 5 minutes. Drain the water and cool. Add the spring onions and tomatoes. You can then pour over the same dressing prepared for the Avocado Salad.
Variation: Instead of the onions and tomatoes you can use chopped flat parsley.

INGREDIENTS:

**1 chopped cucumber
1 tbsp. chopped green capsicum
1 tbsp. chopped yellow
capsicum
1 tbsp. chopped red capsicum
1 tbsp. finely chopped
coriander
1/2 tsp. chilli powder
1 cup (8 oz.) natural yoghurt
1 tsp. ground cumin seeds**

14) Cucumber Raita:
Mix all the ingredients and chill.

INGREDIENTS:
1 chopped apple
55 gm. (2 oz.) seedless grapes
1 chopped plum
1 tbsp. peanuts (boil for 15 minutes)
Seeds from half a pomegranate
2 grated carrots
1 tbsp. chopped coriander
1 tbsp. chopped capsicum
2 tbsp. chopped celery
1 tbsp. chopped fresh fennel
1/2 chopped cucumber
A few leaves of iceberg lettuce, chopped

15) Fruit Raita:
Mix all the ingredients in a large bowl.

For the dressing:
Mix together the natural yoghurt, cumin powder and salt and add these to the fruit and vegetables. Heat the oil and add sesame seeds. Add this to the fruit/vegetable mixture. Stir well, chill and serve.

For the dressing:
4 cups (32 oz.) natural yoghurt
1 tsp. cumin powder
Salt to taste
1 tsp. oil
1 tsp. sesame seeds

INGREDIENTS:
1 lettuce
1 bunch of watercress
1 avocado — sliced (sprinkle with lemon juice to prevent discolouring)
1 clove garlic
2 tbsp. finely chopped chives
Salt and pepper to taste
Juice of 1 lemon
1 tbsp. oil

16) Green Salad:
Wash and prepare the lettuce and watercress. Dry and wrap in a tea towel. Refrigerate until ready to use. Rub the garlic clove in a salad bowl. Arrange the lettuce and watercress in the bowl. Chop garlic finely and mix with the chives. Mix the lemon juice, oil, salt and pepper. Mix the lettuce and watercress with the avocado. Add the lemon and oil dressing and mix well.

INGREDIENTS:
1 ripe avocado
225 gm. (8 oz.) tomatoes
1/2 large cucumber
115 gm. (4 oz.) walnuts
3 large spring onions finely chopped
1 tbsp. chopped chives
1 tbsp. chopped parsley
1 tbsp. oil (or optionally olive oil)
1/2 tbsp. white vinegar
1 1/2 tbsp. tomato puree
1/2 clove crushed garlic
1/2 tsp. tabasco sauce
1 lettuce
Salt and pepper to taste

17) Walnut and Avocado Salad:
Peel and stone the avocado. Chop into pieces. Chop the cucumber, mix into a bowl with the spring onions, parsley, chives and walnuts. Mix oil, vinegar, tomato puree, tabasco, garlic, salt and pepper, and mix with a spoon. Stir this dressing into the above salad. Line a serving bowl with lettuce leaves and pile the salad on top.

INGREDIENTS:

225 gm. (8 oz.) seedless grapes (mixed black and green)
2 oranges
2 bananas
A little lemon juice
1 tbsp. chopped mint
1 lettuce

For the dressing:
1 tbsp. oil
1 tsp. mustard
1 tbsp. vinegar
Salt and pepper to taste
Mix well

18) Florida Salad:

Cut the grapes into halves. Peel the oranges and cut into segments. Peel and slice the bananas. Sprinkle the lemon juice on top. Mix the mint leaves and the dressing. Arrange on washed lettuce leaves.

INGREDIENTS:

115 gm. (4 oz.) peeled and diced cucumber
2 green spring onions chopped
1 tbsp. chopped parsley
4 tbsp. chick-peas cooked and drained
1 avocado — peeled, stoned and sliced

19) Chick-pea Salad:

Mix all the ingredients for the dressing, stir well, and add salt and pepper to taste. Mix the onions, peas, and parsley in a bowl. Chill for a few hours. Add cucumber and avocado. Mix the dressing and pour over the salad when ready to serve.

For the dressing:
1 tbsp. vinegar   1 tbsp. tomato sauce
1 chopped tomato   1 tbsp. tabasco sauce
2 tbsp. oil   Salt and pepper to taste

A FEW TIPS AND SUGGESTIONS:

1. All yoghurt dressings can be stored in an airtight container in a refrigerator for two days.
2. Always sprinkle avocado with lemon juice to avoid discolouration.
3. If the dressing is weak and thick add some more natural yoghurt.
4. Mint juice can be added to a yoghurt dressing if required. (Grind 1 clove of garlic with 2 tablespoons chopped mint. Squeeze out excess moisture and add the moisture to the dressing.)
5. Similarly capsicums may be added: Grind 2 tablespoons chopped capsicums. Squeeze out excess moisture.
6. Most dressings can be prepared a day in advance.
7. Never mix dressings into salads before you are ready to serve, unless the salad is already chilled.
8. Most of the recipes require the yoghurt to be fully drained: Wrap the yoghurt in a muslin cloth and leave it aside for at least 2 hours to allow the water to drain.

3 Napkin Folding

Attractively folded napkins are the cornerstone of a well-set table. The shapes you create must be used to enhance the theme of the table decor you have chosen. To this extent, napkins are more than a convenient way of protecting one's clothes. There are degrees of intricacy with which you can fold napkins, depending upon the occasion. For a family dinner, napkins are simply folded and placed on or beside a plate. Choose your design according to the mood of the table.

The patterns I have chosen are simple to follow. Once you are familiar with them I am sure you will find yourself adding your own variations and experimenting with new ideas. For example, folding two or more napkins of different colours together can give a very special effect.

It is not always necessary to use linen or cloth napkins. I have often found that heavy paper napkins, if crisp and fresh, are easier to handle than linen ones. Furthermore it is not always possible to have linen napkins of the right colour if you wish to match or contrast a particular colour on your table. For more formal dinners, linen napkins are essential. Always make sure that they are clean and uncreased. If lightly starched they will tend to fold more readily and will stay in shape longer.

Other tips to remember are: work on a flat, smooth, hard surface and press firmly when folding the napkins. Try out the pattern first on a napkin that you do not intend to use, before you start on the crisp fresh ones you intend to arrange on the table.

I have set out some of the napkin designs used in the table settings in the book.

1. FLOWER

These folded designs can be used on a plate or as a presentation in a basket liner.
1. Fold the corners of the napkin to the centre.
2. Fold the four new corners again to the centre.
3. Turn the folded napkin over so that the smooth side faces you and the folded corners are facing the table. Fold the four corners to the centre once more. Use a glass or bowl placed in the centre so that the corners do not pull away.

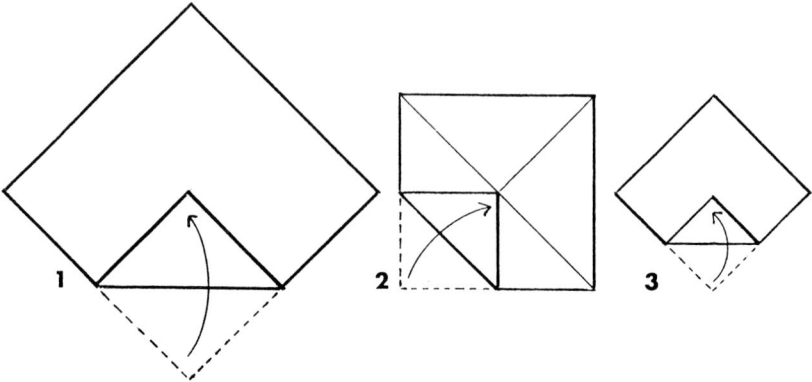

104

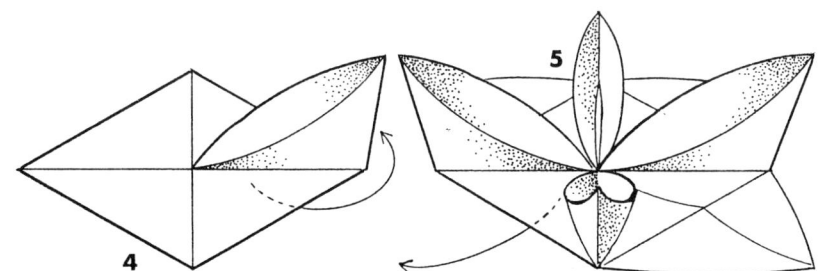

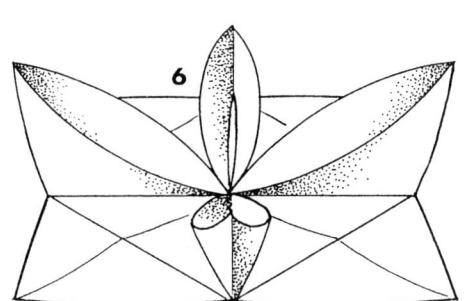

4. Gently pull each of the four corners from underneath and open out.

5. Underneath there are four further corners (the ones folded first). Pull these out gently.

6. The napkin is ready to be placed upon a plate or in a basket.

2. PRINCESS

This can be done in single or double colour.

1. Fold the napkin in half and then each half into accordion pleats as shown. Fold one half under the other.

2. Lift each fold and press down the centre and reverse the crease of each fold to form a triangle.

3. Turn the napkin sideways and fold into accordion pleats as diagram.

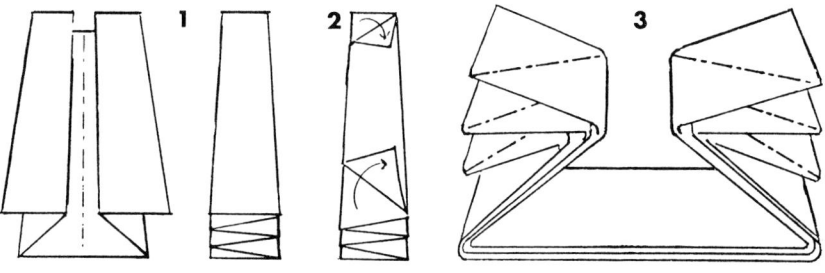

4, 5. Take each corner point ('x') and reverse each fold separately, reversing the crease in the middle of each pleat.

6. Turn the napkin around. It should look as shown.

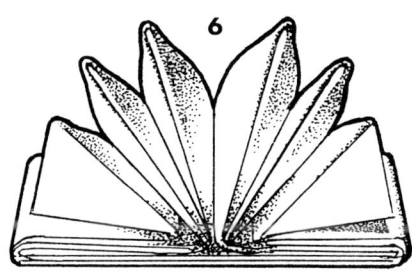

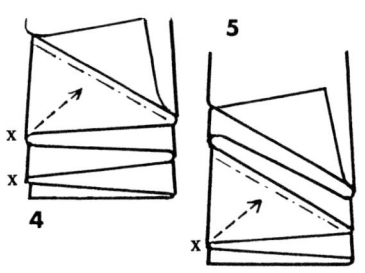

(used on Red and White Table)

3. BIRD OF PARADISE

1. Fold the napkin in half then half again.
2. Fold again diagonally to bring all the single corners to the top.
3. Fold each side inwards to meet in the centre.

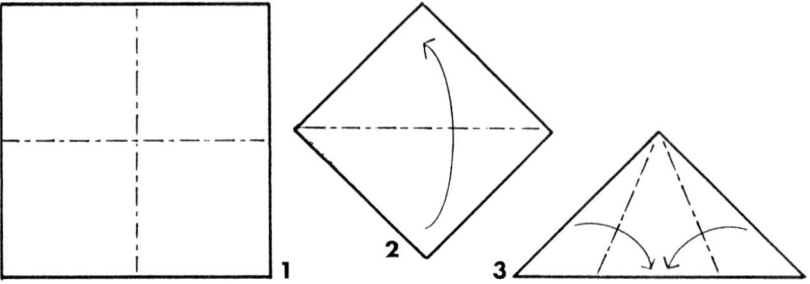

4. Fold 'a' and 'b' underneath and press hard to crease.
5. Fold one half under the other.
6. Lay the smooth edges to the table as shown in the diagram, and pull up one by one the loose corners.
7. The finished napkin will look like the bird of paradise flower.
8. This can be done in double colours.

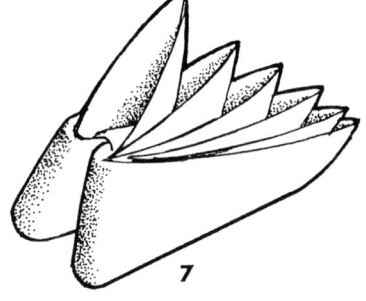

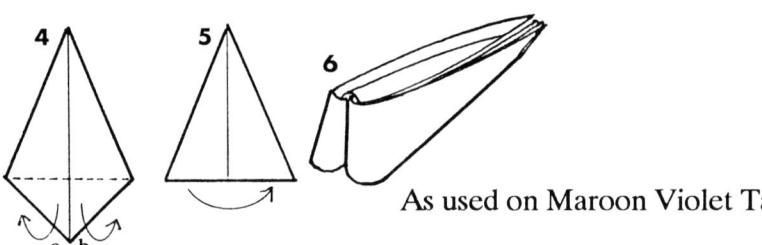

As used on Maroon Violet Table

---

4. BUFFET NAPKIN

1, 2. Open out fully two napkins of different colours. Place one on top of the other. Fold in half then half again as shown.
3. Fold the top loose corner in two thicknesses diagonally to the centre.
4. Fold again on centre line.
5. Fold other two thicknesses as in '3'.
6. Fold again to centre line.
7. Fold the two sides of the napkin underneath.

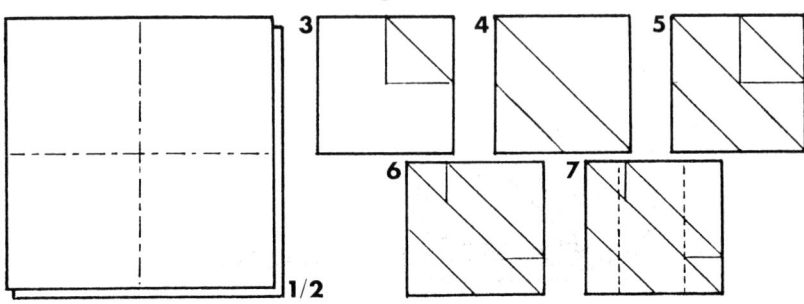

5. THE GLACIER

This napkin fold is very suitable for double colour.
1. Open out two different coloured napkins and place one on top of the other. Fold in half then half again as shown.
2. Fold the top loose corners diagonally in two thicknesses only.
3. Take the same two thicknesses and make creases from the
4. You will see a zigzag pattern as shown. Fold the napkin in half diagonally.
5. Turn points 'c' and 'd' under and tuck in. Clip if using a paper napkin.

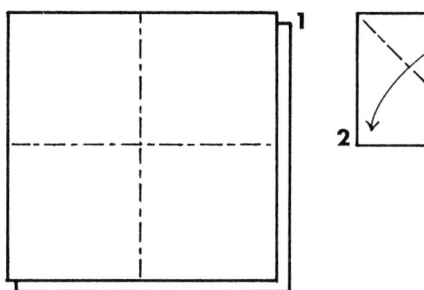
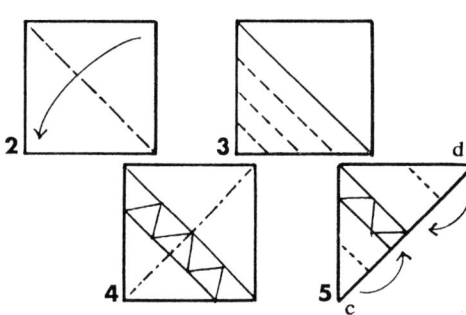

As shown on Sunset Table.

6. LILY

This folded napkin is made in single colour.
1. Fold the napkin in half diagonally then fold each corner again into the centre.
2. Take points 'a' and 'b' and fold on dotted line.
3. Fold the top corner down on dotted line.
4. Fold again on line 'c'.
5. Take points 'd' and 'e' behind and tuck into each other.

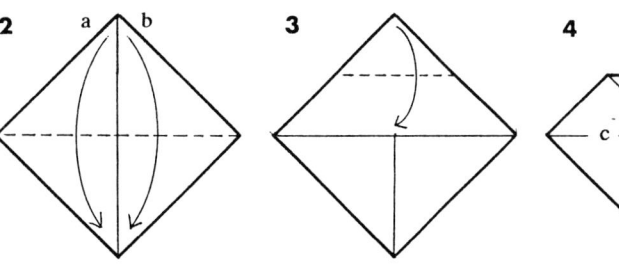

6. Turn the napkin upside down to bring collar at the bottom.
7. Tuck both the loose corners 'a' and 'b' down behind the collar.

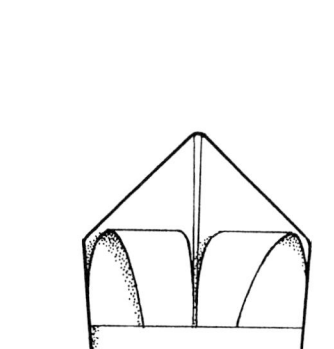

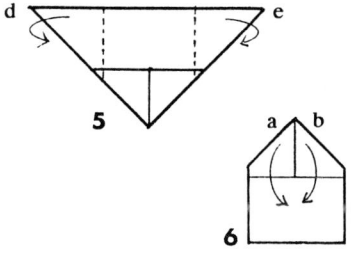

As shown on Pineapple Table.

7. SPOON HOLDER

This fold can be done in single or double colour.
1. Fold the napkin in half, then half again. Put the loose corners to the top.
2. Take the top loose corner and fold it down to the bottom.
3. Take the next corner and fold it down about 1.5 cm above the first.
4. Take the third corner and fold down similarly about 1.5 cm above the second.

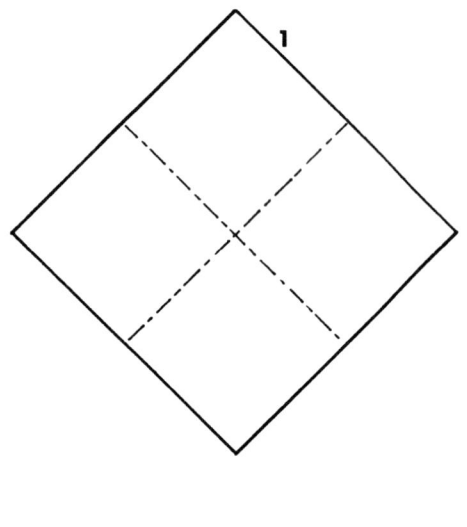

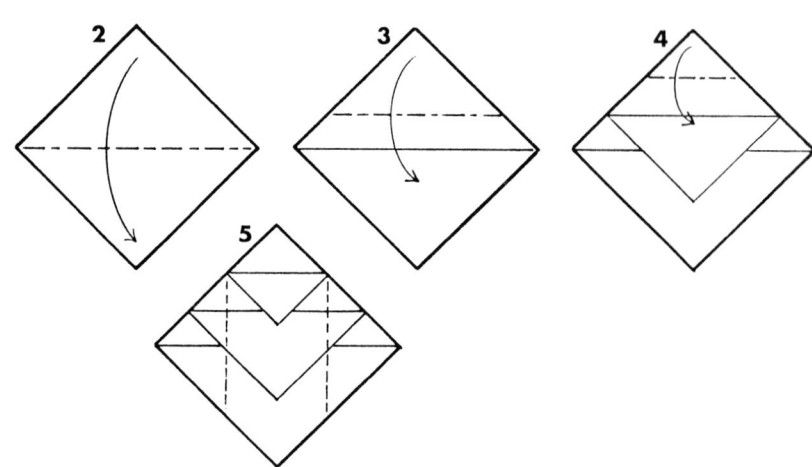

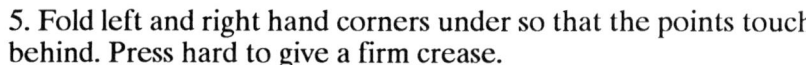

5. Fold left and right hand corners under so that the points touch behind. Press hard to give a firm crease.
6. You now have a pocket at line 'e-e' in which to place your silver.

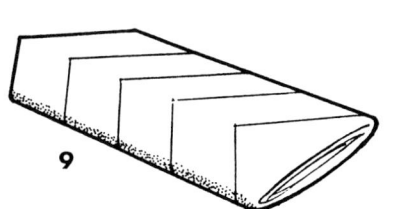

As shown on Daffodil Table.

8. CARD HOLDER

Repeat steps 1-4 of previous fold (spoon holder). Continue as follows:
5. Fold up top loose corner about 2.5 cm from previous fold.
6. Repeat with next two corners.
7. Fold up bottom corner similarly.
8. Fold left and right hand corners under.
You now have a napkin like a card holder and you can place a greetings card in one of the pockets.

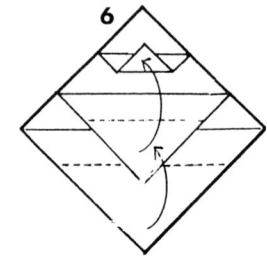

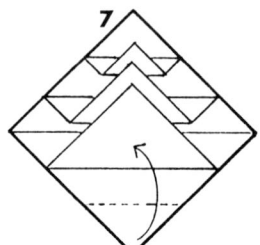

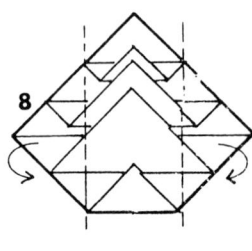

As shown on Silver Anniversary Table.

9. THE WATERFALL

Upright and falling creases.
1. Fold the napkin in half diagonally.
2. Fold up point 'b', making the crease 'a-a' about two thirds of the total width.
3. Pleat vertically in approx. 2 cm pleats.
4. Place in a glass, allowing the outer corners to overhang.

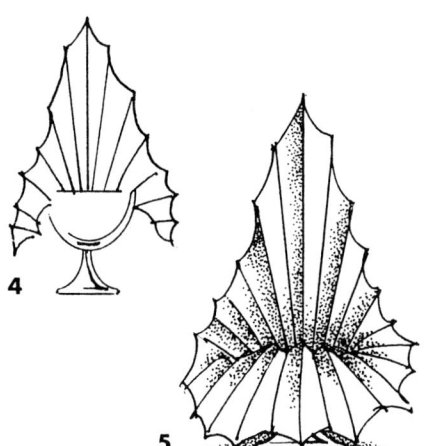

4

5

As shown on Sunflower Table.

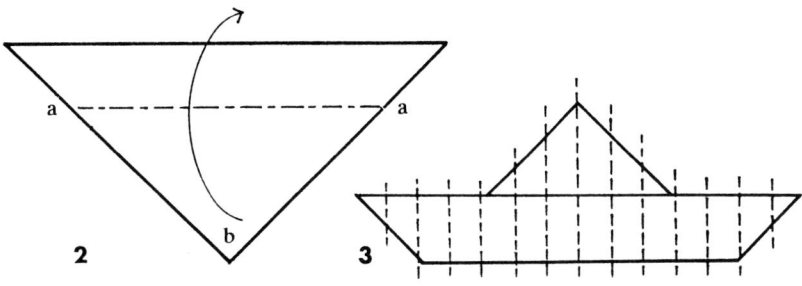

5. Pull down the front layer of the napkin to cover the glass and most of its stem.
You can do this in double colours so that the central flap shows in a different colour.

10. CANDLE

1. Fold in half diagonally.
2. Fold up bottom edge about 2-4 cm.
3. Roll up, showing the bottom fold outside.

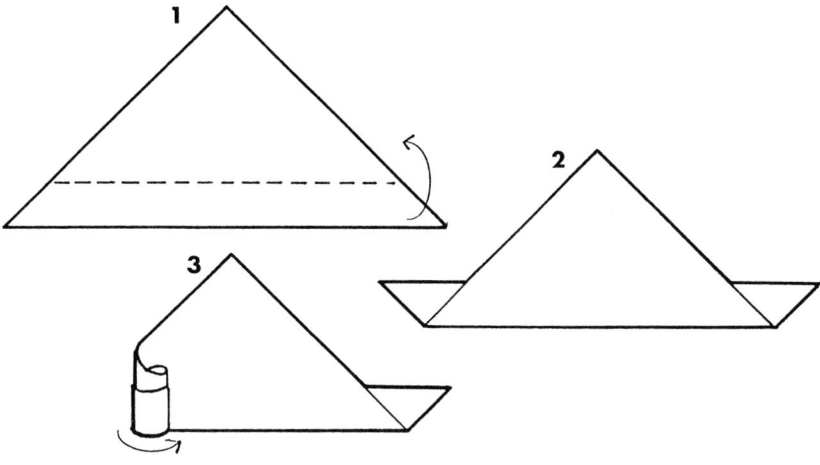

4. Tuck the end in so that the 'candle' will stand up.

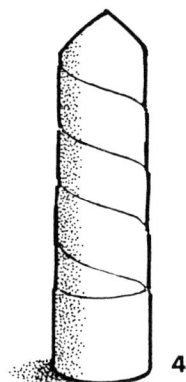

4

As shown on Crystal Table.

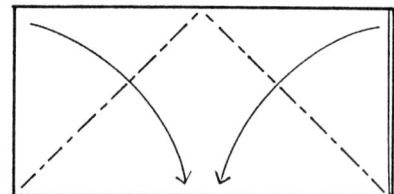

11. PALM LEAF

1. Fold the napkin in half.
2. Fold the two loose outer corners diagonally to the centre.
3. Turn the napkin over and fold the flap down to the base.

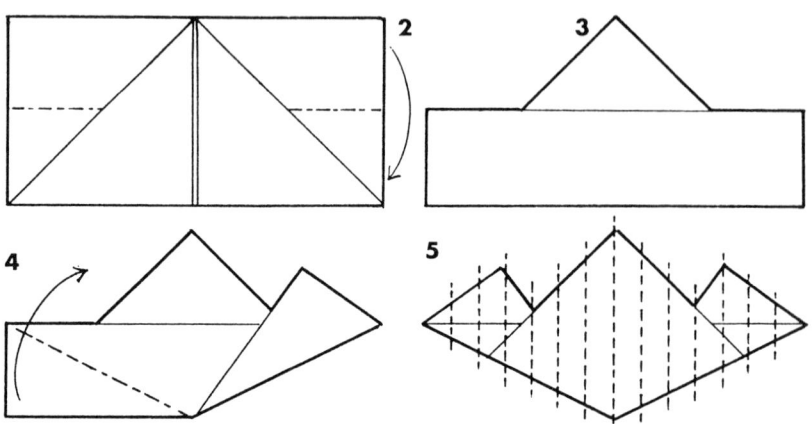

4. Fold up the bottom corners as shown.
5. Turn over and make pleats of 1.5 cm or more (depending upon the size of the napkin) at each side of the centre. Press all creases sharply.
6. Napkin will look like diagram when placed in a ring.

As used on Daisy Table.

12. PALM LEAF (2nd style)

1. Fold in half diagonally.
2. Fold up the corners as shown.

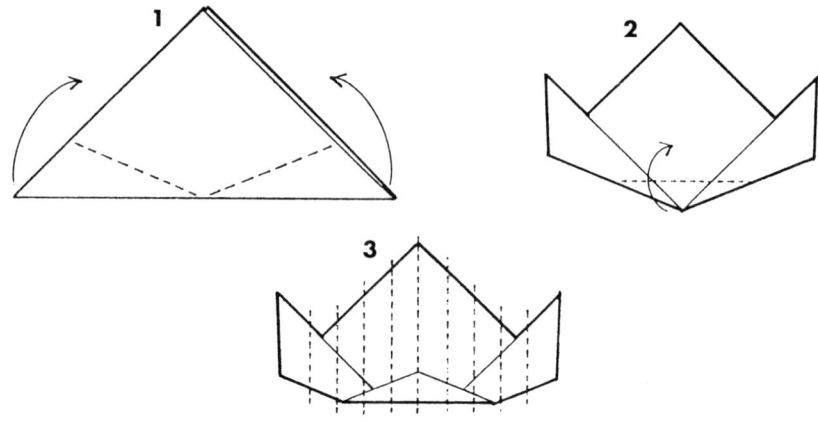

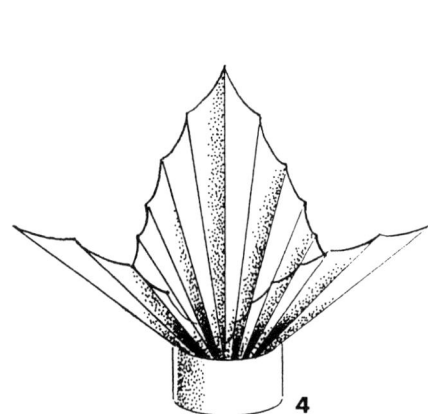

3. Fold up the bottom corner about 5 cm.
4. Fold the napkin in half and make pleats on each side of 1 to 3 cm. Place in a glass.

As used on Royal Table and Moon Table.

13. DROOPING PALM LEAF

1. Fold in half diagonally.
2. Fold up bottom edge as shown.
3. Fold down top edge, then pleat as previous napkin.

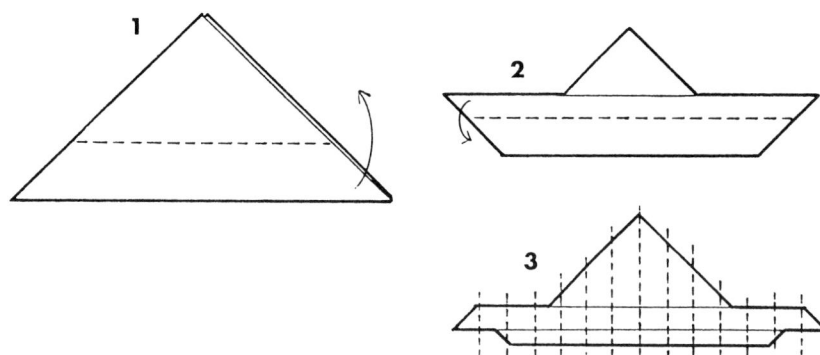

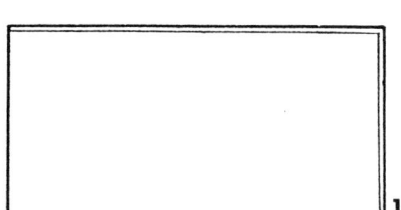

Use on cocktail tables.

4. Place bottom of pleated napkin in a glass and open out upper part. The ends will drop as shown in the diagram.

14. RAINBOW FAN

This design was used on the Anthurium Table in dark green and red. It looks better in two colours.

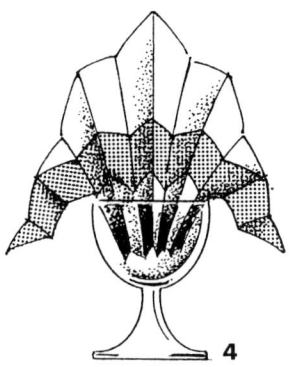

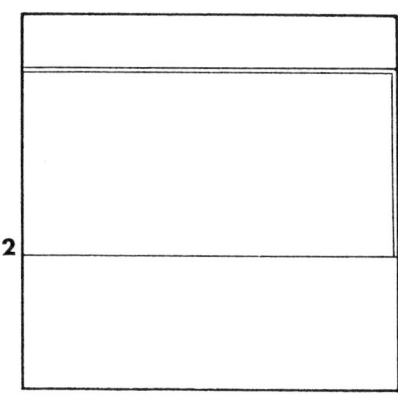

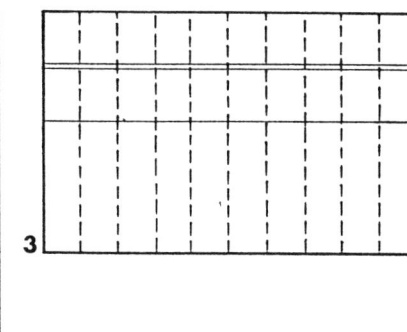

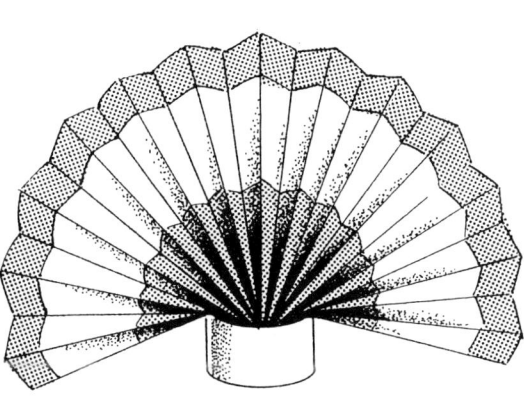

1. Fold the first napkin in half to form a rectangle.
2. Place on different coloured napkin leaving top edge about 2.5 cm higher.
3. Fold up lower edge as in the diagram.
4. Pleat from left to right.
Now repeat the above with a further two napkins, and put the two folded pairs together.
5. As one pair will form about a quarter circle, two pairs are joined to get a half circle.
6. Place in a napkin ring and open out the pleats to form a half-circle.

15. PEACOCK FAN

This design is shown on the Peacock Table in dark green and light blue.

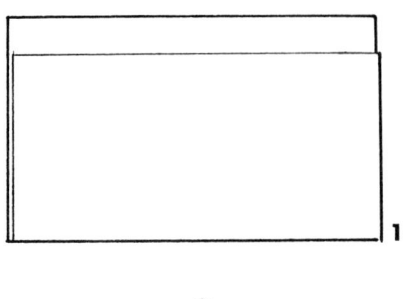

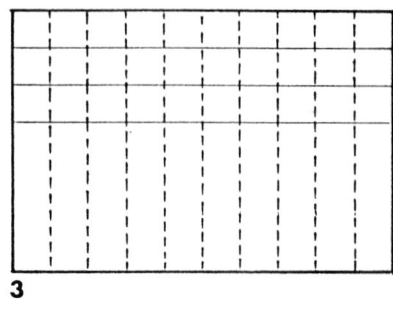

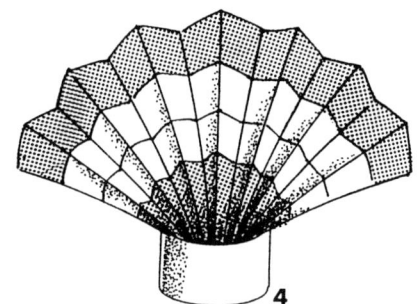

1. Fold light coloured napkin in two so that about 2.5 cm shows at top.
2. Place on darker napkin to show further 2.5 cm at top.
3. Fold up bottom edge of darker napkin. You will now have four edges at top. Pleat from left to right.
4. Place in a napkin ring as shown. Decorate with a peacock feather if desired.

16. FLYING BIRD or BIRD OF PARADISE

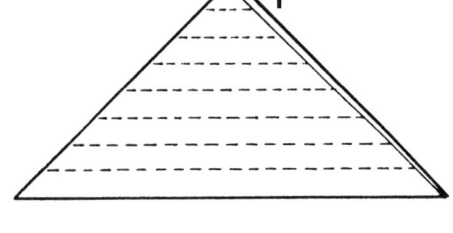

Used on the Bandhani Table
1. Fold in half diagonally.
2. Pleat from bottom to top.
3. Fold in the centre, taking both ends to top and keeping longer ends to the outside.
4. Place in a napkin ring and open out. It will look like the wings of a flying bird.

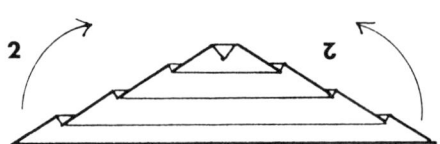

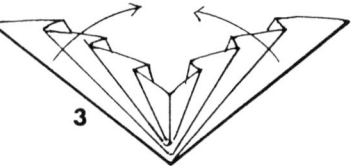

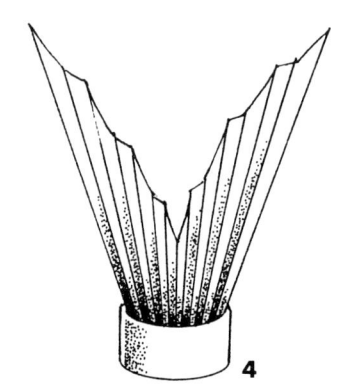

NB. If you would like to make this in two colours take another napkin and fold as in 1 and 2 above. Then place on top of the first, keeping longer ends inside, and fold both up together.

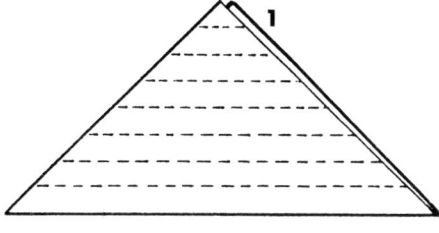

17. THE LEAVES

1. Fold in half diagonally.
2. Pleat from bottom to top.

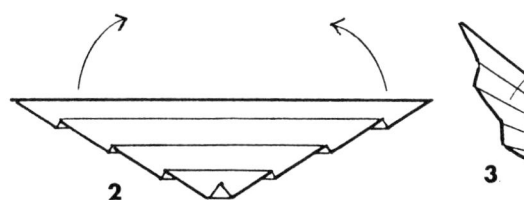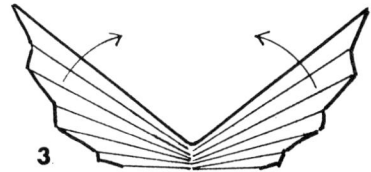

3. Fold in the centre, taking both ends to the top and keeping longer ends to the inside.
4. As this fold has a flat base it can be used either standing or laid down.
5. This can be used either standing or laid down. As used in Rose Table.

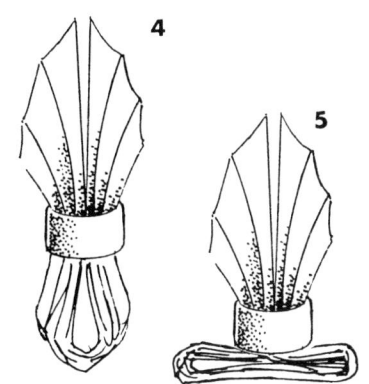

18. THE ROSE

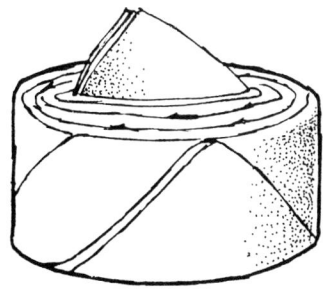

1. Fold the napkin as in steps 1 and 2 of the previous design (the Leaves), but miss out the final pleat so that a small triangular piece remains standing out.
2. Roll the pleated napkin with the plain surface inside. Tuck the end into one of the pleats to prevent the roll from opening.
This design can be used in mixed colours as shown in the illustration of the Rose Table.

Cocktails

EXOTIC COCKTAILS (NON-ALCOHOLIC)

The idea of cocktails is a relatively modern phenomenon. The United States of America is considered the original home of cocktails although they are enjoyed the world over and cover an enormous range of mixes.

A cocktail can be short and strong or long and weak. The joy of making a cocktail is akin to that of cooking. You should allow your imagination to develop new variations, and create different combinations.

Juices may be mixed directly in the glass, then shaken or stirred. Ice can also be made colourful by adding a few drops of food colour or adding pieces of fruit to the ice tray.

Some useful suggestions:
a) Crushed Ice:
Place ice cubes in a napkin and gently crush with a mallet.
b) Cocktail Glasses:
Use either long-stemmed glasses or small juice glasses. Make sure the glass is never filled right to the top. Always allow room for the ice to melt.
c) Where black salt is used, only use a pinch as an optional.
d) In all drinks you can use sugar or honey to sweeten and salt to taste.

1) POMEGRANATE JUICE:

Cut the required number of pomegranates in half, crosswise. Extract the juice by squeezing over a lemon juicer. Discard the pulp and seeds. To make a punch with this juice as a base add water, sugar, salt, pepper, cumin powder, and 'black salt' (optional) according to taste.

2) MILK SHAKES:

General hints: To sweeten always use raw cane sugar or honey. Garnish the milk shake or cocktail glass with an array of fresh fruit, or use sprigs of leaves, e.g. herbs, fresh mint, etc. The aim is to make the drink look attractive, and to tempt the palate. Make sure the fruit is thoroughly washed before use. Milk shakes and cocktails are better served with straws. Paper parasols may be used as a garnish. Kiwi fruit also makes a delicious garnish.

INGREDIENTS:
2 small apples
3 cups chilled milk
4 individual apple slices
Sugar to taste.

A) Apple Milk Shake:
Peel and core the apples. Grate in a liquidizer, then add milk and sugar and liquidize until smooth. Serve in a glass using the apple slices to garnish.
Variation: You can mix apples and nectarines, or apples and pears. Serves 4.

INGREDIENTS:
2 apricots
1¹/₂ cups chilled milk
4 almonds

B) Apricot Milk Shake:
Soak the almonds for 10 minutes in warm water. Peel and liquidize together with chopped apricot and milk. Add sugar to taste and serve.
Serves 4.

INGREDIENTS:
4 tbsp. chopped pineapple
1 banana peeled and chopped
1¹/₂ cups chilled milk
6 tbsp. single cream
Sugar or honey to taste
Crushed ice

C) Caribbean Milk Shake:
Liquidize all the ingredients. Serve in a balloon glass with plenty of crushed ice, and garnish with pineapple.
Serves 2-3.

INGREDIENTS:
1 cup (8 oz.) diced melon
2 cups chilled milk
A few melon balls to garnish
Sugar or honey to taste

D) Melon Milk Shake:
Liquidize all the ingredients (except the melon balls) and serve in tall glasses garnished with the melon balls, and with straws and/or cocktail spoons.
Serves 2-3.

INGREDIENTS:
1 nectarine
10 sliced strawberries
2 cups chilled milk
Sugar or honey to taste

E) Nectarine and Strawberry Milk Shake:
Liquidize all the ingredients and strain. Pour into tall glasses and garnish.
Serves 2-3.

INGREDIENTS:
2 peaches
2 cups chilled milk
2 tbsp. vanilla ice-cream
Sugar or honey to taste

F) Peach and Vanilla Milk Shake:
Boil the peaches in boiling water for one minute. Peel and stone. Mix the peaches, milk, sugar and ice-cream and blend in an liquidizer. Pour into glasses and garnish.
Serves 2-3.

INGREDIENTS:
1 custard apple
1¹/₂ cups chilled milk
Sugar to taste
A pinch of cardamom powder

G) Custard Apple Milk Shake:
This makes a delicious drink! Pulp the custard apple in a large strainer, extracting the seeds and then mashing them, either by hand or with the back of a spoon. Liquidize the mashed custard apple and the remaining ingredients. Pour into tall glasses, add cardamom powder and serve.
Serves 2-3.

INGREDIENTS:
225 gm. (8 oz.) of lychees
2 cups of chilled milk
1 tbsp. vanilla ice-cream
Sugar or honey to taste

H) Lychee Milk Shake:
Peel and stone the lychees. Mix with the ice-cream, milk and sugar. Blend in a liquidizer. Pour into glasses, garnish and serve.
Serves 2-3.

3) FRUIT PUNCHES:

General: Passion-fruit is a tropical fruit, grown in East Africa, South America and the Caribbean. It has a delicious flavour and the pulpy juice can be added to any punch.

INGREDIENTS:
- 1 cup pineapple juice
- 1 cup orange juice
- 1 cup red grapefruit juice
- Pineapple slices to garnish
- Sugar or honey to taste
- Crushed ice

A) Caribbean Punch:
Mix all the juice. Put some crushed ice into tall glasses. Add the juice and decorate with slices of pineapple. Serve with cocktail straws or spoons.
Serves 2-3.

INGREDIENTS:
- 1 ripe mango
- Juice of 1 lemon
- 1 small bottle of soda water
- Sugar or honey to taste

B) Mango Punch:
Peel and chop the mango. Add the remaining ingredients and liquidize. Garnish and serve.
Serves 2-3.

INGREDIENTS:
- 3 dl. ($^1/_2$ pint) fresh mandarin juice
- 1 tbsp. pineapple juice
- 1 banana
- Sugar or honey to taste

C) Mandarin Punch:
Mix both juices and the banana and liquidize until smooth. Pour the mixture into tall glasses, garnish and serve.
Serves 3-4.

INGREDIENTS:
- 2 nectarines or 1 mango or 2 peaches
- $1^1/_2$ cups orange juice
- $^1/_2$ cup (4 oz.) raspberries
- 1 tbsp. clear honey
- Crushed ice

D) Nectarine Punch:
Slice the nectarines, add the orange juice, liquidize and strain. Wash the raspberries thoroughly, then liquidize with honey.
To serve: Pour the nectarine and orange juice into a glass partially filled with crushed ice. Slowly pour the raspberry juice over the cocktail, allowing it to sink to the bottom of the glass. Stir very gently, then garnish as required.
Serves 3-4.

INGREDIENTS:
- 10 strawberries
- 1 banana peeled and sliced
- $1^1/_2$ cups pineapple juice

E) Strawberry and Pineapple Punch:
Mix strawberries, banana and pineapple juice. Blend in a liquidizer. Strain the mixture. Pour into tall glasses and garnish with herb leaves or strawberries.
Serves 3-4.

INGREDIENTS:
- $1^1/_2$ cups sparkling grape juice
- Juice of 1 lime
- A piece of fresh pineapple (diced)
- 1 mango (diced)

F) Grape Punch:
Mix the grape juice and lime juice. Pour into glasses. Add pieces of pineapple and mango, and serve with cocktail spoons.
Serves 3-4.

INGREDIENTS:
Juice of 2 passion-fruits
1 1/2 cups orange juice
2 peaches
6 tsp. sugar

INGREDIENTS:
15-20 strawberries
1 cup chilled pineapple juice
1/2 cup chilled white grape juice
Sugar or honey to taste

INGREDIENTS:
1 1/2 cups fresh chilled coconut milk
1 cup (8 oz.) chopped pineapple
2 tsp. fresh lime juice
Sugar or honey to taste
Ingredients for coconut milk:
1 fresh coconut grated
3 cups boiling water

INGREDIENTS:
4 apricots
3/4 cup chilled pineapple juice
3/4 cup chilled orange juice
4 tbsp. fresh single cream
Sugar or honey to taste

INGREDIENTS:
Juice of 2 limes
2 cups pineapple juice
4 slices of fresh pineapple, finely chopped
8-10 fresh cherries, stoned
Sugar or honey to taste

INGREDIENTS:
1/2 a large melon
2 apples
115 gm. (4 oz.) seedless grapes
2 tbsp. lime cordial (use Rose Cordial)
Pulp from 5 passion-fruits (remove seeds)
pinch of Black Salt (optional)
1/2 tsp. ground cumin powder
Sugar to taste
2 glasses water, salt and pepper to taste

G) Passion-fruit and Peach Punch:
Boil the peaches in boiling water for 1 minute. Peel and stone. Mix the juices and the peaches and liquidize. Add sugar to taste. Strain and serve with suitable garnish.
Serves 3-4.

H) Strawberry Punch:
Mix the juices, strawberries and sugar and liquidize. Strain. Pour into glasses, garnish and serve.
Serves 3-4.

I) Coconut Punch:
Mix the coconut milk, pineapple juice, sugar and lime juice and liquidize. Strain. Pour into glasses, garnish and serve with crushed ice.

For the coconut milk:
Mix together the grated coconut and boiling water, liquidize, strain and chill.
Serves 3-4.

J) Apricot Punch:
Stone the apricots. Mix the juices, cream and apricot and liquidize. Pour the mixture into glasses, garnish and serve.
Serves 3-4.

K) Pineapple Punch:
Mix the lime and pineapple juice. Pour into glasses, add pieces of pineapple and cherries. Serve with cocktail straws and spoons. Variation: Instead of pineapple pieces, you can use mango, nectarine or peach pieces.
Serves 3-4.

L) Fresh Fruit Punch:
Peel and dice the melon and apples. Liquidize all the ingredients. Strain and chill. Pour into glasses and garnish. Add more water as required. As sizes of melon differ, taste and adjust as required.
Serves 10-15.

INGREDIENTS:

1 pineapple, diced
3 glasses of water
Juice from 3 pomegranates
Pulp from 5 passion-fruits
(remove seeds)
1 tbsp. mint liqueur
Sugar, salt, cumin powder,
a pinch of Black Salt

INGREDIENTS:

3 apples
4 passion-fruits (pulped and
de-seeded)
1 ripe mango
1 tbsp. pomegranate syrup
2-3 glasses water
Salt, sugar, black pepper,
black salt, cumin powder to
taste

INGREDIENTS:

2 peaches
2 nectarines
10 plums
1 pomegranate
2 apples
225 gm. (8 oz.) grapes
3 tbsp. lime cordial
2-3 glasses water
Sugar, salt, cumin powder,
black salt and pepper to
taste

INGREDIENTS:

1/2 a large melon
1 pomegranate
2 apples
Juice of 2 lemons
2 tbsp. ginger juice
3 tbsp. pomegranate syrup
Sugar, salt, cumin powder,
black salt and pepper to
taste
2-3 glasses water

M) Passion Punch:
Liquidize all the ingredients and chill. Garnish when ready to serve.
Serves 5-6.

N) Passion/Apple Punch:
Prepare fruit, liquidize, chill and serve with garnish.
Serves 5-6.

O) Peach Nectar Punch:
Prepare the fruit according to type. Liquidize, chill and garnish when ready to serve.
Serves 5-6.

P) Ginger/Melon Punch:
Prepare fruit according to type, blend in a liquidizer, chill and garnish before serving.
Serves 10-15.
Note: To make ginger juice, grate a small piece of ginger, add half a cup of water, liquidize and strain.

INGREDIENTS:
  1 pineapple, diced
  Juice of 2 pomegranates
  Juice of 1 lemon
  3 glasses water
  Sugar, salt, black salt,
  cumin powder and pepper to
  taste

Q) Tangy Pineapple Punch:
Blend in a liquidizer, chill and serve with garnish.
Serves 10-15.

INGREDIENTS:
  1 large melon, diced
  Juice of 2 lemons (or lime
  cordial)
  2 tbsp. ginger juice
  2-3 glasses water (or as
  required)
  Sugar, salt, pepper, cumin
  powder to taste
  Black salt.

R) Tangy Melon Punch:
Liquidize, strain, chill and garnish before serving.
Serves 15-20.

INGREDIENTS:
  450 gm. (1 lb.) lychees (peeled
  and de-seeded)
  225 gm. (8 oz.) washed
  strawberries
  4 tbsp. lime cordial
  2-3 glasses water
  Sugar

S) Lychee and Strawberry Punch:
Liquidize, chill and garnish before serving.
Serves 10-15.

INGREDIENTS:
  Pulp from 2 ripe mangoes
  450 gm. (1 lb.) grapes
  3 apples, peeled and diced
  Juice of 2 lemons
  2 tbsp. ginger juice
  2-3 glasses water
  Salt, sugar, cumin powder,
  pepper to taste

T) Mango Punch:
Liquidize, chill and garnish before serving.
Serves 15-20.

INGREDIENTS:
  Pulp from 10 passion-fruits
  Juice of 2 pomegranates
  1 pineapple, diced
  225 gm. (8 oz.) lychees
  (deseeded)
  2-3 glasses water
  Sugar, salt, cumin powder
  and pepper to taste

U) Mixed Tropical Fruit Punch:
Liquidize, chill and garnish before serving.
Serves 10-15.

INGREDIENTS:
----

450 gm. (1 lb.) lychees
(deseeded)
3 glasses cream soda
2 tbsp. vanilla ice-cream

INGREDIENTS:
----

4 unripe mangoes
55 gm. (2 oz.) chopped walnuts
6 cups water
Fresh single cream (optional)
Sugar, salt, pepper and cumin
powder to taste
Black salt

INGREDIENTS:
----

1 medium-sized water melon
1 cup passion-fruit juice
1 cup grape juice
1 tbsp. lemon juice
1 tbsp. ginger juice
3 tbsp. lime cordial
1 tbsp. peppermint liqueur
(optional)
Salt, sugar, pepper, and
black salt to taste
Melon balls to garnish

INGREDIENTS:

Juice of 1 pineapple
Juice of 1 mango
1 cup grape juice
Juice of 6 apples
Juice of 1 lemon
1 tbsp. ginger juice
1 grated apple
Salt, pepper, sugar and
cumin powder to taste

V) Creamy Lychee Punch:
Blend in a liquidizer, chill and serve with garnish.
Serves 10-15.

W) Mango Sherbet:
Cook the mangoes in steam, cool, peel and liquidize. Add water to dilute. Season, stir and strain. Cool, add chopped walnuts. Pour into individual glasses, whirl over 1 teaspoon cream. (You can leave out the cream if you prefer.)
Serves 6-8.

X) Melon Punch:
Blend all the ingredients in a liquidizer. Cool and serve with garnish.
Serves 10-15.

Y) Pineapple Punch (Version 2):
Blend all the ingredients in a liquidizer. Serve chilled with garnish.
Serves 10-15.

GENERAL TIPS FOR PUNCHES:
Most of the above mixes should make 10-15 glasses. This will however depend on the size of the glasses and size and juice content of the fruit, and should therefore always be tasted. Use 'sea salt' sparingly and only if required. Add more water if required. Strain the punch whenever possible. Plums, peaches and nectarines should be boiled for 1 minute in boiling water, before pulping. Use seedless grapes, whenever possible. Always strain the liquidized pulp of passion-fruit.

INGREDIENTS:
1¹/₂ cups pineapple juice
3 tbsp. cream of coconut
3 large scoops of vanilla
ice-cream

4) CREAMY PINA COLADA:
Mix all the ingredients, and liquidize until smooth. Pour into glasses and serve immediately with crushed ice.
Serves 3-4.

5) YOGHURT DRINKS:
General: To make yoghurt drink base, use natural yoghurt. Wrap the yoghurt in a muslin cloth and keep aside for at least three hours to allow the water to drain out.

INGREDIENTS:
225 gm. (8 oz.) raspberries
1 cup (8 oz.) chilled natural yoghurt
¹/₂ cup chilled milk
Sugar or honey to taste

A) Raspberry Drink:
Mix all the ingredients and liquidize until smooth. Pour into glasses, garnish and serve.
Serves 2-3.

INGREDIENTS:
2 peaches
¹/₂ cup chilled milk
1 cup (8 oz.) natural yoghurt
Sugar or honey to taste

B) Peach Drink:
Boil peaches in boiling water for 1 minute. Peel and stone. Mix all the remaining ingredients with the peaches, liquidize and serve.
Serves 2-3.

INGREDIENTS:
225 gm. (8 oz.) strawberries
1¹/₂ cups chilled red grape juice
2 tbsp. clear honey
2 tbsp. chilled natural yoghurt

C) Yoghurt Cocktail:
Thoroughly clean the strawberries, add the grape juice, yoghurt and honey and liquidize until smooth. Strain the mixture. Pour into glasses, garnish and serve.
Serves 2-3.

INGREDIENTS:
1 banana
1 apple
1¹/₂ cups (12 oz.) natural yoghurt
4 tsp. honey or sugar

D) Banana and Apple Drink:
Peel and chop the banana and apple. Add yoghurt and honey and liquidize. Pour into glasses, garnish and serve.
Serves 2-3.

INGREDIENTS:
1 cup (8 oz.) strawberries
³/₄ cup pineapple juice
1 cup (8 oz.) natural yoghurt
Sugar or honey to taste

E) Strawberry and Pineapple Drink:
Mix all the ingredients and liquidize until smooth. Strain, pour into glasses, garnish and serve.
Serves 2-3.

INGREDIENTS:
1 cup red grape juice
1 cup (8 oz.) natural yoghurt
1 tbsp. extra yoghurt
Sugar or honey to taste

F) Grape Drink:
Mix all the ingredients and liquidize until smooth. Pour into glasses. Spoon the extra yoghurt on top, garnish and serve.
Serves 2-3.

INGREDIENTS:

2 peaches
1/2 cup pineapple juice
1 cup (8 oz.) natural yoghurt
Sugar or honey to taste

INGREDIENTS:

4 apricots
1½ cups chilled fresh orange
juice
4 tbsp. natural yoghurt
Sugar or honey to taste
Slices of pistachio and
almonds for garnish

INGREDIENTS:

1/2 cup cold milk
1/4 cup (2 oz.) strawberry
syrup
4 scoops of strawberry
ice-cream
1 small bottle cold club soda
3 tbsp. whipped cream
Mixed fruit to garnish
Sugar or honey to taste

INGREDIENTS:

1 cup (8 oz.) strawberries
2 cups (16 oz.) natural
yoghurt (remove excess
moisture)
3/4 cup (6 oz.) sugar, or to taste

INGREDIENTS:

2 large ripe peeled avocados
1/4 cup lemon juice
2 cups orange juice
1 cup (8 oz.) sugar or to taste
2 cups (16 oz.) natural
yoghurt (remove excess
moisture)

G) Peach and Pineapple Drink:
Mix all the ingredients and liquidize until smooth. Pour into glasses, garnish and serve.
Serves 2-3.

H) Apricot and Orange Drink:
Boil the apricots in boiling water for 1 minute. Peel and stone them. Add the orange juice and sugar and liquidize. Beat the yoghurt with a spoon. Pour the juice into glasses. Spoon the yoghurt over the juice. The yoghurt should float on top. Garnish with almonds and pistachio.
Serves 2-3.

6) STRAWBERRY DRINK:

Mix the milk and strawberry syrup. Pour into tall glasses. Add a scoop of ice-cream. Pour on a small amount of soda. Press the ice-cream and soda together with a spoon. Add a second scoop of ice-cream. Fill the glass with soda. Garnish with cream and fruit. Serve immediately.
Variation: Raspberry Drink — use raspberry syrup and vanilla ice-cream. Chocolate Drink — use chocolate syrup and chocolate ice-cream.
Serves 2-3.

7) FROZEN YOGHURTS:

A) Strawberry Yoghurt:
Wash strawberries and discard tops. Make a puree in a blender. Stir the yoghurt in until smooth. Mix the sugar, puree and yoghurt and stir well. Freeze in an ice-cream container.
Variation: Use raspberries, pineapple, peaches or plums instead of strawberries.

B) Avocado Yoghurt:
Mash and puree the avocado. Mix the lemon, orange juice and sugar and keep aside. Stir the yoghurt until smooth. Mix all the ingredients. Place in a freezer for 3-5 hours. Stir twice with a wooden spoon while freezing. For a smooth texture, break into small pieces, beat with a spoon or liquidize, until fluffy. Refreeze for a further 3-5 hours.
Serves 4-5.

Appendix

PART I

VEGETABLE FLORISTRY

A) GENERAL: USING FRUIT AND VEGETABLES FOR DECORATION

Using fruit and vegetables as a decorative medium can be creative, fun and novel. There is no limit to what you can design, and it need never be boring or repetitive.

Fruit and vegetables can either be placed on the table to eat as a salad, or can be merely decorative. They are never wasted, as they can be re-used the next day.

Flower shapes and bouquets are my favourite designs. The vase for a bouquet can be any suitable container, even a basket. Alternatively, you can make your own vase from a large fruit or vegetable.

One can even make a mini-garden by creating trees and branches. Adding greenery not only establishes colour but also produces a large and spectacular arrangement.

When shopping, look at the different fruits and vegetables on offer and think how you can transform them into different designs.

Creative designs enhance the beauty of fruits and vegetables. All one does by cutting and arranging them is to add to this quality. The secret of making your design look fresh and remain crunchy is to keep the cut shapes in ice cold water. An hour before required, remove them from the water and arrange. Spray iced water over them before serving to retain freshness.

CUTTING VEGETABLES AND FRUIT INTO FLOWERS:
Vegetables or fruit are often displayed in their original shapes or cut into geometric shapes, however one can cut them into beautiful flower shapes, or any other designs, according to one's own inventiveness. Vegetables can be cut and arranged to resemble a particular flower, or a tree with branches, or a garden.

For all vegetable floristry you will need:
Container or vase
Sharp knife, e.g. a paring knife
Bowl of cold water to chill (helps flowers 'bloom')
Melon scoop
Toothpicks
Biscuit or cookie cutters in flower shapes
Scissors
Oasis
Pin holders
Grapefruit knife

Use silver vases when decorating for an Anniversary Party or similar occasion.

B) SPECIAL VEGETABLE CUTTINGS/FLORISTRY:

1. Vegetable leaves

Leeks: Leeks are shaped for use as 'stalks'. You can either keep the leek whole or cut the outside leaves in two vertical strips (up to half the length from the top) so that it can bend easily. Leeks can be make to stand upright by fixing on to a pin holder. If this is kept in cold water for a few hours, the leaves will curl attractively. The whole leek can be placed in the centre of the arrangement as a tree on which vegetable flowers and fruits can be arranged with a toothpick.

Celery: Choose crisp celery with branches and leaves. This can be used whole, as for the leek, to look like a tree. Alternatively you can cut each celery stick vertically (up to half the length from the top) and arrange on to a pin holder to look like a plant or a tree. Bend the celery leaves slightly from the bottom (without breaking) to cover a wider area. These strips can then be eaten with a dip, or used as a base for arranging vegetable flowers using toothpicks.

Rhubarb: Rhubarb is an extremely attractive vegetable because of its contrasting red and green colour. Cut the rhubarb into 2 or 3 strips about 8-10 cm. from the top. Do not cut through to the bottom. Place them in cold water and refrigerate. Arrange on a pin holder or oasis and arrange vegetable flowers on it using toothpicks.

Saragva sing: This is an Indian vegetable resembling a long green twig. It is normally cooked with gram flour. Place in a bowl of cold water to crisp. Arrange in an oasis or pin holder, and use as above.

2. Vegetable Foliage or Greenery:

Parsley: Parsley has a deep green colour and has been traditionally used in Western cooking for garnishing. Parsley bunches are an easy and effective form of foliage or background greenery.

Watercress: The leaves are a delicate dark green and are about 5-7 cm. long. They can be used as fillers in smaller arrangements, especially those with a large quantity of small bright flowers.

Mint leaves: Mint leaves have a deep green colour and a refreshing fragrance. As the leaves are small, multi-stemmed leaves should be used in decoration.

Green cabbage, and all kinds of lettuce: Buy fresh green cabbage or lettuce. Keep them in a bowl of cold water and make them crisper by placing in a refrigerator. Some lettuce leaves have brownish tips with a greenish core. This looks particularly effective in arrangements.

Other lettuce and leaves you can use: Spinach, Roman lettuce, Dandelion green, Lamb's lettuce, Little Gem lettuce, broccoli, flowering cabbage, etc.

3. Colour combinations for floristry:
Red: Tomatoes, red peppers, beetroot, and strawberries.
Yellow: Yellow peppers, yellow cucumber, turmeric powder in cooked foods or for colouring vegetables.
Orange: Carrots, kumquats, turmeric and red food colour mixed to colour vegetables.
White: White radish, turnips, onions, baby corn.
Deep red and purple: Red cabbage, beetroot and black grapes.
Green: Green chillies, peppers, peas, lettuce, parsley, celery, cabbage leaves, mint leaves, bay leaves, etc.
Some vegetables particularly suitable for decoration:
Cherry tomatoes, cranberries, olives, peas in pods, ginger roots (as stems), coloured chillies, baby corn, mange-tout, and the root of fennel.

RED CAPSICUM FLOWER
The red flower which has been used on the Anthurium Table is one of the most beautiful, and is made from red peppers, more commonly known as red capsicum.
1. Cut several slices from the pepper.
2. Using the natural shape of the top of the pepper, cut into the shape of a heart.
3. Select a long, red chilli, and push a toothpick into the stem end.
4. Push the toothpick, with the chilli, into the rounded top of the 'heart'.

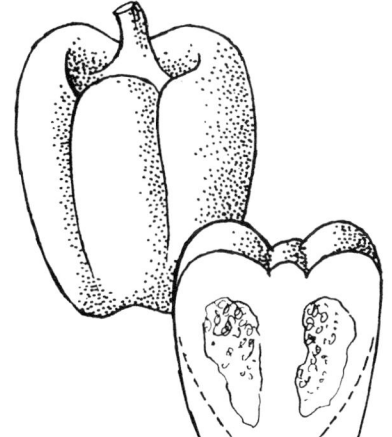

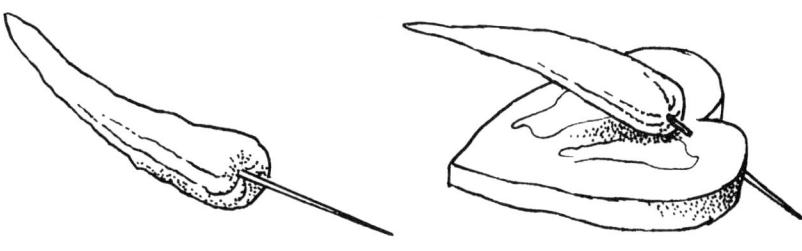

TOMATO SUNFLOWER
1. Choose a round tomato, and remove three-quarters of the skin, starting at the base.
2. Turn the tomato upside down and make four cuts across the top.
3. Carefully separate the eight 'petals'.
Use to garnish any dish.

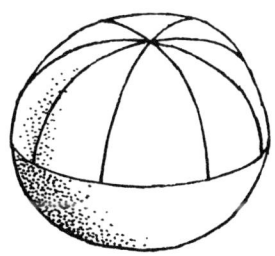

125

CARROT OR RADISH FLOWERS
1. If using radish, choose a long one. Make a point at one end.
2. With a sharp knife, cut petal shapes. Do not cut right through.
3. Put the knife at an angle and cut off the flower.
4. Repeat, making as many flowers as needed.
5. Put the flowers in ice water in the fridge for one hour.
6. Use any small fruit or vegetable to make centre of flower and pierce with a toothpick.

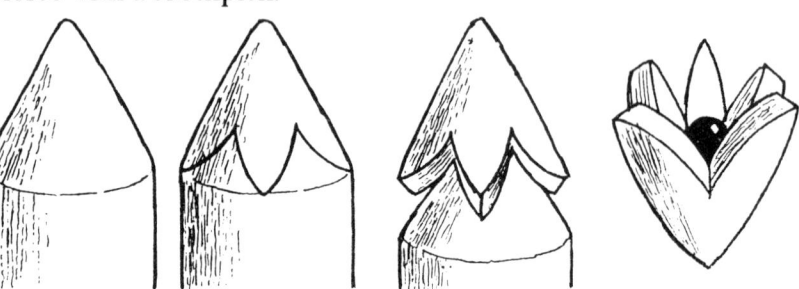

As used on Red and White Table.

WHITE RADISH OR EGG PLANT FLOWER
1. Using a very long radish, cut to about 8 cm.
2. With a very sharp knife, cut a thin sheet from the radish.
3. Putting the sheet on a cutting board, make parallel cuts as shown in the diagram.
4. Fold in half and then into a cylinder.
5. Secure with a rubber band or a toothpick.

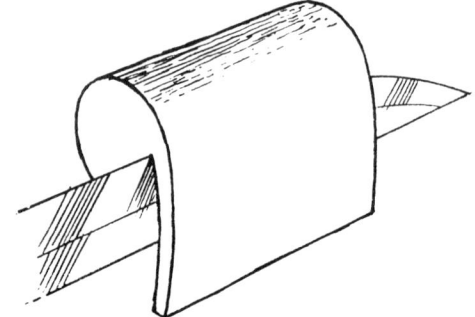 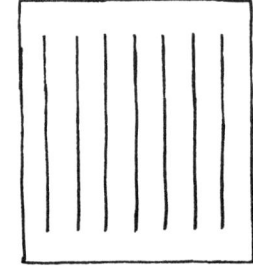 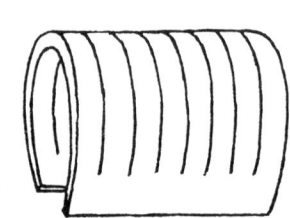 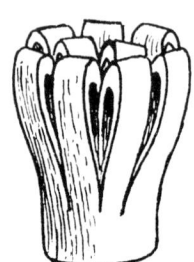

ONION OR RED RADISH FLOWER
1. Choose a rounded shape. If using onion, cut off the top.
2. Cut deeply a zigzag pattern all round.
3. Separate the two halves, place in ice water, and refrigerate for three to four hours.
4. Soak in diluted food colouring of your choice.

 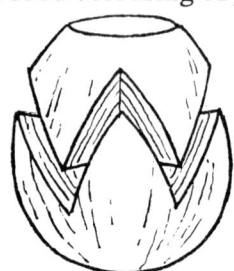 

ONION FLOWERS

1. Peel the onion and cut off the top.
2. Cut petal shapes into the outer layer, and remove the upper section.
3. Open up the first layer slightly so that the next layer is exposed, and cut petals into the next layer, discarding the upper section as before.
4. Continue until only the centre bit is left.
5. Cut a criss-cross pattern into the centre.
6. Refrigerate in iced water for three to four hours to enable the flower to 'bloom'.

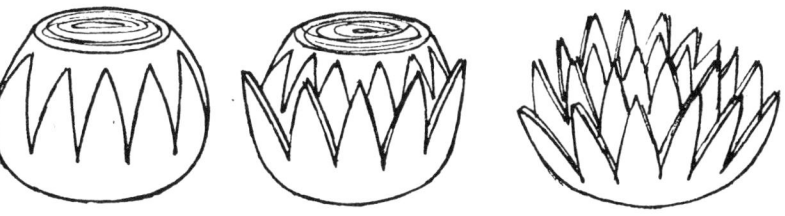

As used in Onion Flower arrangement (Photo on page 130)

WHITE RADISH FLOWER

1. Peel the radish and cut to about 10 cm.
2. The petals are made by cutting slices lengthways from both sides. The petals will get narrower as the radish gets smaller.
3. Dip into iced water to curl them. (Coloured blue on Peacock Table.)
4. Make a base for the flower by cutting a section from the radish, and insert a toothpick.
5. Beginning with the largest strip, stick the petals onto the toothpick, each petal being at right angles to the previous one.
6. In the centre put a section of radish, cutting the surface in a criss-cross pattern.

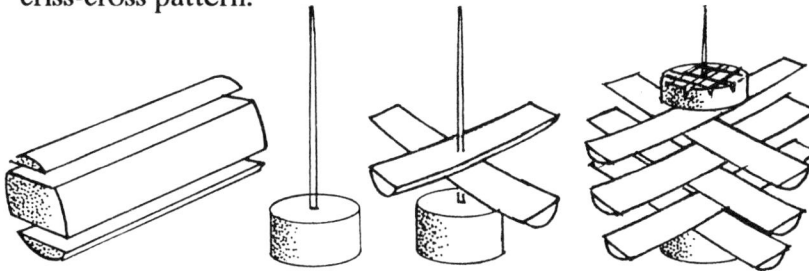

This flower has been used on the Peacock Table. Beetroot or carrot could be used in the same way.

ONION FLOWERS
Note: the flowers can be made from any size of onion.
1. Peel the onion, leaving the root end intact.
2. Make a vertical cut down through the centre, making sure that you do not cut right through.
3. Repeat the cut at right angles to the first, then diagonally.
4. Refrigerate in iced water for three to four hours.

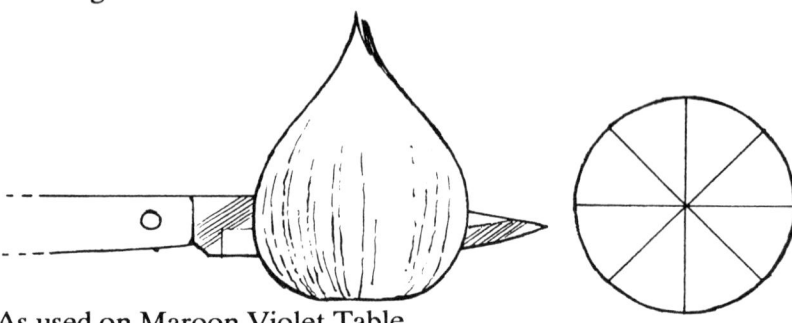

As used on Maroon Violet Table.

BEETROOT, TURNIP OR CARROT FLOWER
1. Peel and cut into thin slices.
2. Cut each slice into a petal shape — they can be pointed or rounded as you wish.
3. Leave the petals in iced water for three to four hours to make them curl.
4. Stick the petals onto a toothpick, piercing each one close to one end and allowing the toothpick to show through like a stamen.

(As used on the Pineapple Table)

PARSNIP FLOWER
1. Peel the parsnip and cut thin slices from the widest part.
2. Curl a slice into a cone shape and place a baby corn in the centre to make a stamen.
3. Secure by inserting a toothpick through the petal and the baby corn.
4. Dip into iced water for crispness, and arrange in a bouquet.

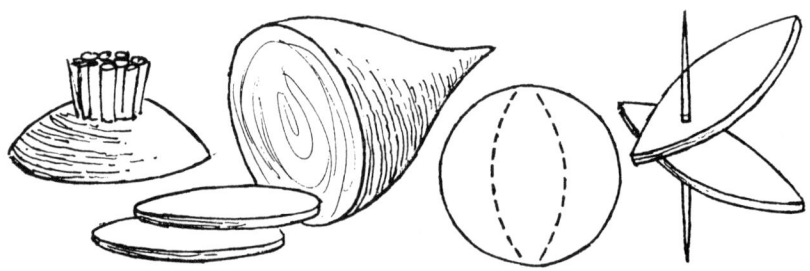

(As used in the Vegetable Bouquet)

**A SAMPLE DISPLAY OF
VEGETABLE FLORISTRY AND FOOD DESIGN**

a-Onion and radish arrangement
b-Turnip flower arrangement
c-Exotic salad
d-Coconut and pistachio sandesh
e-Blue radish flower vase

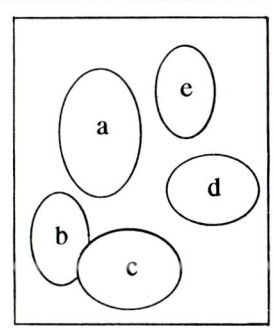

ONION FLOWER ARRANGEMENT

CHICORY FLOWER

VEGETABLE FLOWER BOUQUET

BEETROOT TULIPS
1. Select a long beetroot and peel it.
2. With the point of a sharp knife, make two cuts as shown in the diagram.
3. Repeat on the other side of the beetroot, and try to keep an equal space between the cuts.
4. Using a grapefruit knife, cut out the centre.

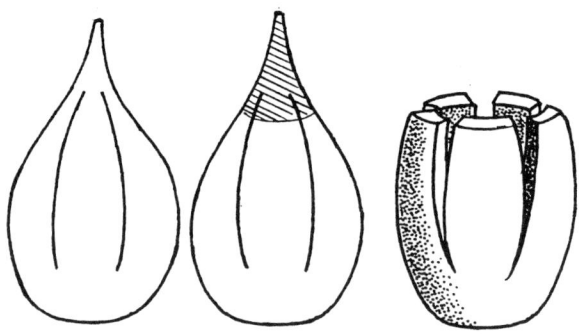

As used in Vegetable Bouquet.

ONION FLOWERS
1. Choose a long onion.
2. At the pointed end, cut a zigzag pattern.
3. Peel off separate layers from the top. Each layer makes a flower.
4. Place a small fruit or vegetable in the centre of each flower and attach with a toothpick.

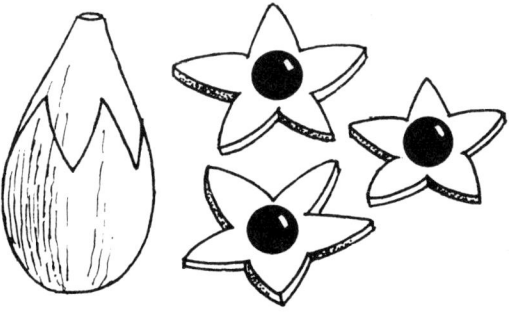

(As used on Crystal Table and Maroon Violet Table)

RADISH FAN
1. Choose a long radish and trim off the root end.
2. Make vertical cuts along the length.
3. Refrigerate in iced water for three to four hours to open out.

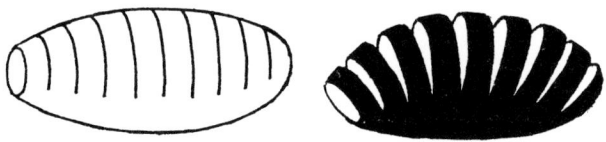

(As used on the Moon Table)

RADISH BLOSSOM
1. Choose a round radish and hold it with the root end downwards.
2. Make a series of deep cuts across.
3. Turn and make a further series of cuts at right angles.
4. Dip in water and refrigerate for three to four hours.
5. Stick onto a toothpick and arrange into a bouquet.

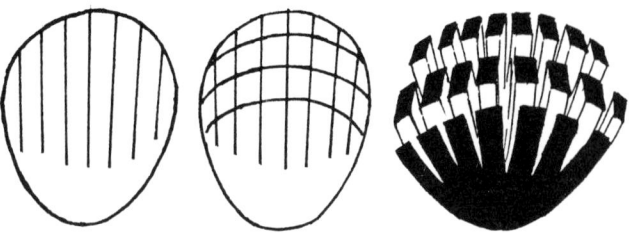

(As used on the Moon Table)

TURNIP ROSE
1. Peel a round turnip, slice off the top.
2. Cut petal shapes as shown and cut off the surrounding area.
3. Cut larger, thicker petals outside the first ones and cut off the surrounding area again.
4. Repeat as required depending on size of turnip.
5. Immerse in diluted food colouring and refrigerate for three to four hours.

(Rose Table)

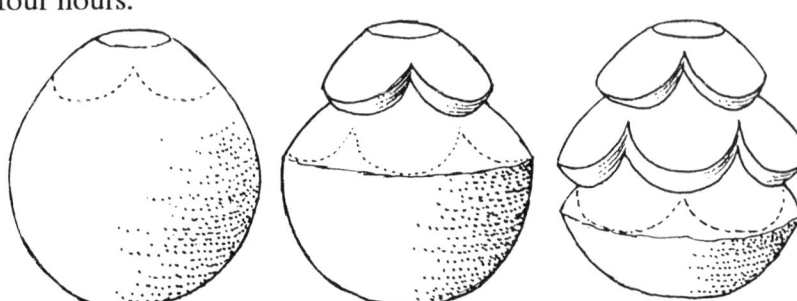

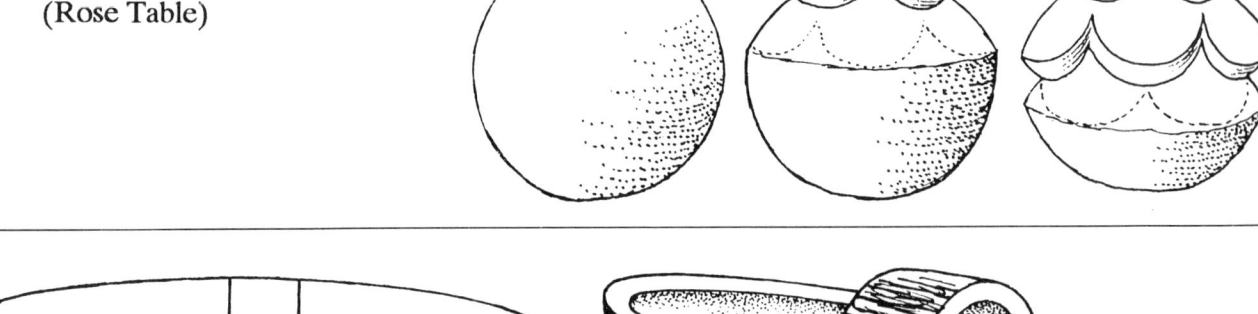

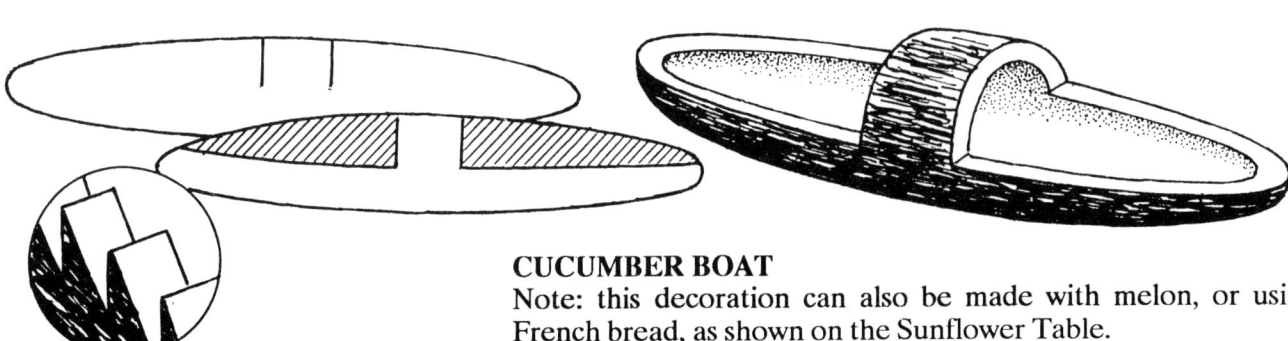

CUCUMBER BOAT
Note: this decoration can also be made with melon, or using French bread, as shown on the Sunflower Table.
1. Make two vertical cuts in the centre.
2. Remove the shaded portion.
3. Scoop out the inside of the boat and the inside of the handle.
4. Cut a jagged edge along the edges as shown.

Making the boatman.
1. Cut a lengthwise slice of carrot and round off the top.
2. Make cuts for the arms and legs.
3. Cut a thin strip of carrot for an oar.

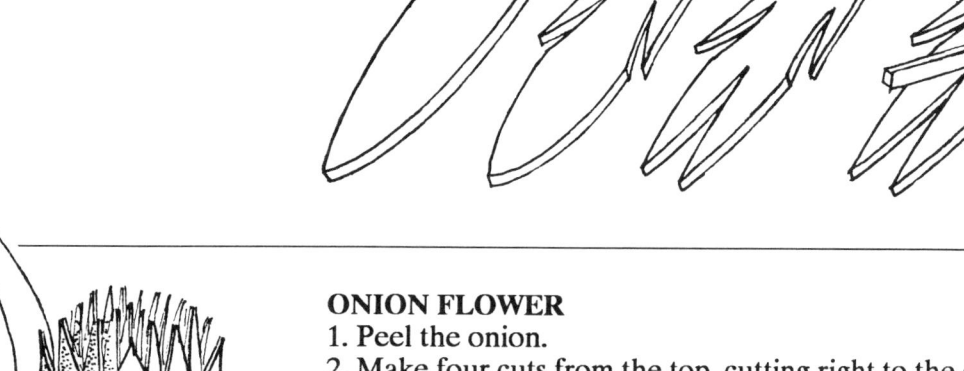

ONION FLOWER
1. Peel the onion.
2. Make four cuts from the top, cutting right to the centre.
3. Separate the petals slightly, place in water and refrigerate for three to four hours to enable the flower to bloom.

(As used in Onion Flower arrangement)

ONION FLOWER
1. Peel the onion.
2. Cut a deep zigzag pattern at one end and remove the shaded area.
3. Lengthen the cuts.
4. Open the flower slightly and refrigerate as before.

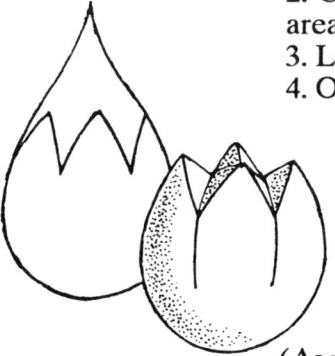

(As used on Maroon Violet Table)

RED RADISH FLOWER (1)
1. Cut a deep zigzag pattern around the radish.
2. Separate the two halves, making two flowers.

(Moon Table)

RED RADISH FLOWER (2)
Make four deep cuts into the sides of the radish as shown.

SPRING ONION FLOWER
1. Cut off the leaves.
2. Make deep cuts into the onion as shown in the diagram.
3. Open slightly and refrigerate for three to four hours to allow the petals to curl.

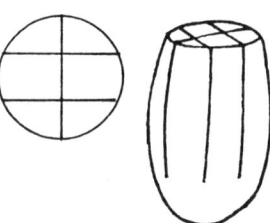

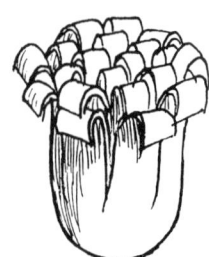

(shown in the Onion Vase, coloured yellow)

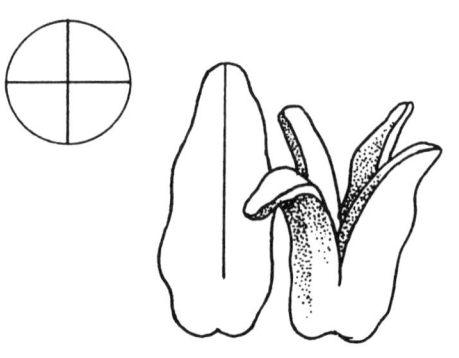

RED CHILLI FLOWERS
1. Choose short chillies.
2. Make two cross cuts down from the top as shown.
3. Open slightly, refrigerate for three to four hours.

(as used on the potato cake on the Anthurium Table as well as on Chilli Tree on Brown and Gold Table.)

TURNIP FLOWER
1. Peel the turnip and place upside down (i.e. root on top)
2. Cut long thin petal shapes around the base and cut away above them.
3. Cut a second row of petals above the first, cut away above.
4. Repeat this process until the whole turnip has been used.

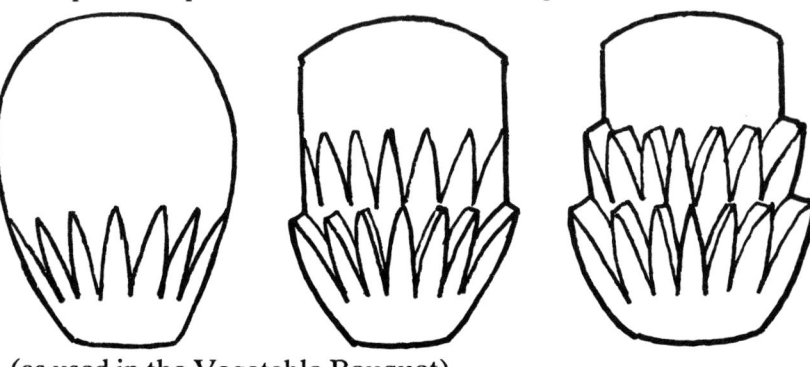

(as used in the Vegetable Bouquet)

WHITE RADISH FLOWER/ROSE
1. Peel and cut off 3 to 5 cms.
2. Cut a criss-cross pattern deeply into the top.
3. Make sloping cuts into the side of the radish.
4. From the remaining radish cut thin slices and insert them into the sloping cuts.
Refrigerate as before.

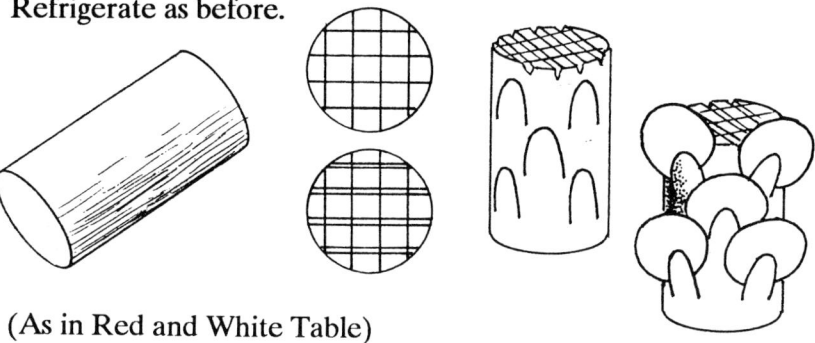

(As in Red and White Table)

CARROT FLOWERS
1. Take approximately half a carrot and trim the ends square.
2. Make deep vee-cuts down the length of the carrot as shown.
3. Cut slices off to make flowers; put on toothpicks.

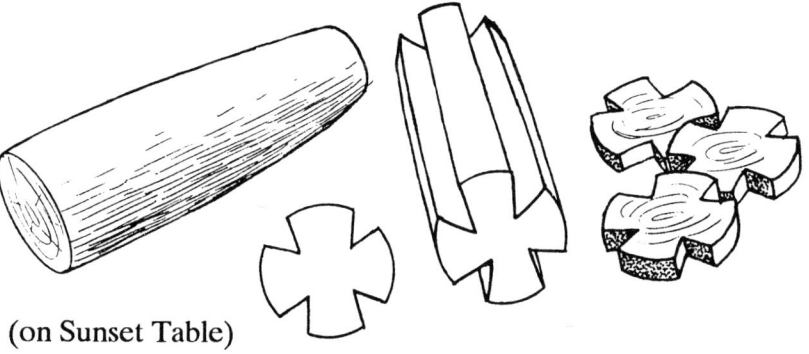

(on Sunset Table)

TURNIP FLOWER
1. Peel the turnip and cut slices.
2. Cut flower shapes from the slices.

(See sample display of Vegetable Floristry and Food Design, page 129)

ONION FLOWER

1. Peel the onion.
2. Cut petal pattern on base of onion, cutting through one layer only, and peel off layer above the cuts.
3. Cut further petal shapes above the first and peel off again.
4. Continue until you reach the top.
5. This flower can be used face up or face down.

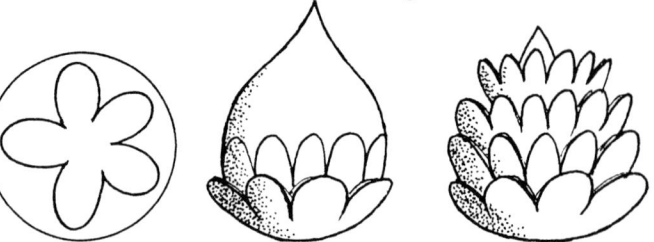

(See sample display of Vegetable Floristry and Food Design, page 129)

CUCUMBER LEAVES

Note: these can also be made from melon)
1. Cut off long strips of the cucumber skin, with a little flesh underneath, and trim into a leaf shape.
2. Along the edges make vee cuts.
3. Cut out a thin strip along the centre of the leaf.
4. Make similar cuts for the veins.
(These leaves have been used in the onion vase)

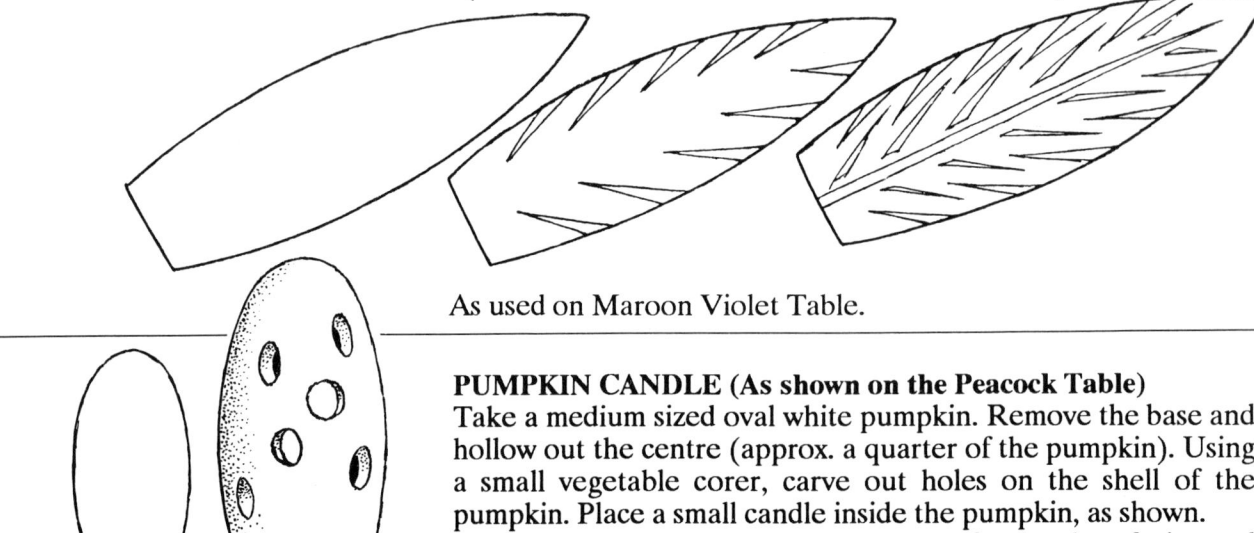

As used on Maroon Violet Table.

PUMPKIN CANDLE (As shown on the Peacock Table)

Take a medium sized oval white pumpkin. Remove the base and hollow out the centre (approx. a quarter of the pumpkin). Using a small vegetable corer, carve out holes on the shell of the pumpkin. Place a small candle inside the pumpkin, as shown.
In the same way, you make a candle from other fruits and vegetables, e.g. melon, pineapple, papaya.

CHICORY FLOWER (As shown in the Chicory Flower arrangement)

Take a medium sized Chicory and gently separate the petals. Place in a bowl of ice cold water for a few hours. Arrange on a vase, as shown.

PART II	SOME BASIC COMMONLY-USED INGREDIENTS

INGREDIENTS:

    6 sticks of cinnamon
    6 cloves

A) Garam Masala:
Grind all the ingredients to form a fine powder. Use in cooking, preferably freshly ground. You can make garam masala in larger quantities and store in an airtight container for a few months.

INGREDIENTS:

    55 gm. (2 oz.) of rice for each serving.

B) Rice:
Place the rice in a sieve and rinse thoroughly with cold water. Drain well. Place some water in a pan (double the volume of the uncooked rice). Put the water to boil — add $1/2$ teaspoon of lemon juice and 1 teaspoon of butter. When boiling, add the rice. Bring to boil again, stir once and cook uncovered on a low heat for 15-18 minutes or until the grains are tender (not mushy). Basmati rice has a thinner, longer, more pointed grain. Use this rice to give authenticity to curries, pilau and other Indian dishes. (Uncle Ben's long grain rice is a good substitute.)

INGREDIENTS:

    900 gm. (2 lb.) of butter
    Few drops of lemon juice.

C) Ghee:
Melt the butter in a saucepan on medium heat. Allow it to simmer until a clear, yellowish liquid is formed and a sediment settles in the base of the pan. (This should take approximately 25 minutes.) Add the lemon juice. Carefully strain the clarified butter through a muslin cloth, making sure all the sediment has been removed. Pour the ghee into a container with a close-fitting cover. It will store for quite a long time in a covered container.

INGREDIENTS:

    4 pints of full cream milk (red top milk)
    $1/2$ tsp. citric acid or lemon juice

D) Mava:
Boil the milk until it thickens (like porridge). Add the milk powder 5 minutes before removing the milk from the heat. Stir continuously so the milk at the bottom of the pan does not burn. After removing the pan from the heat, continue stirring slowly for another 10 minutes and then set aside to cool. Mava can be prepared in advance and frozen. Ready-made Mava is available in Indian grocery/sweetmeat shops.

INGREDIENTS:

    To make 450 gm. (1 lb.) of mava:
    4 pints of milk (red top)
    4 tbsp. of milk powder

E) Paneer (Chhanno):
Boil the milk in a pan stirring constantly. Add citric acid or lemon juice. The milk will curdle in a few minutes. Remove pan from the heat and allow it to cool for about 20 minutes. Then remove the solid substance by filtering through a muslin or other thin cloth. Knot the ends of the cloth (containing the semi-solid curdled milk) and place the bag under cold running water to remove all excess particles. Allow the bag to drain for a while to remove all the excess moisture. Alternatively, place the bag in another container and weight it down to force all the moisture out. The remaining solid substance is known as chhanno and is used in making Bengali sweets such as Rasgoola, Rasmalai and Chum Chum.
Makes two cups of Paneer.

INGREDIENTS:

340 gm. (12 oz.) ground almonds
115 gm. (4 oz.) caster sugar
115 gm. (4 oz.) icing sugar
5 tbsp. condensed milk
1 tsp. lemon juice
Few drops vanilla and almond essence

F) Marzipan:

Sieve the ground almonds and caster sugar until well mixed and even. Add the icing sugar, flavouring, condensed milk and lemon juice. Mix thoroughly using a wooden spoon, and knead. Then wrap the mixture in plastic film or place in an airtight container. This will prevent the moisture from evaporating. The paste would otherwise become hard and difficult to use.

G) Natural food colours (for vegetable flowers):
a) Red or pink
Soak a boiled beetroot in a bowl of water for a few hours to release the colour, or grate the beetroot and extract the juice for a deeper red or purplish colour. Use strawberries, raspberries and redcurrants in the same way as the beetroot for a lighter, more pinkish colour. Red Cabbage: Boil, liquidize and strain the coloured water.
b) Blue
Use blueberries — liquidize directly and strain the coloured water.
c) Yellow
Use turmeric — add half a teaspoon of turmeric to a bowl of water.

INGREDIENTS:

1/2 cup water
1 cup (8 oz.) sugar

H) Syrup:

Boil the water, then add the sugar. Stir and continue boiling until completely dissolved. 'One taar' syrup is a thin consistency. 'Two taar' syrup is a medium thick consistency. 'Three taar' syrup is a very thick consistency.

INGREDIENTS:

2 cups (16 oz.) yoghurt
Salt to taste
Cumin powder

I) Raita:

Beat the yoghurt thoroughly. Stir in salt and cumin powder.
Variations: For cucumber raita, add grated cucumber. For fruit raita, add mixed finely-chopped fruit. The basic raita serves 3-4.

J) Green Chutney: see Recipe no.23.

PART III	SOME HELPFUL HINTS AND TIPS

1) How to keep herbs and spices in good condition:
Store them in a cool place, e.g. a shelf or sideboard, away from direct sunlight. Screw lids on tightly after use. Keep away from steam as this may cause the spices to solidify at the bottom of the jars. If unsure about the freshness of your spices, smell them. If the aroma is not very strong they need to be used quickly. (Note: spices do not go 'off', they just become ineffective.)

2) Potatoes:
There are several types of potatoes — choose according to the requirements of the recipe. Remove potatoes from their polythene bags to avoid 'sweating'. Store potatoes in the dark as light turns them green.

3) Almonds:
There are two types of almonds: bitter and sweet. The bitter almond is used for making almond essence and skin oil. Sweet almonds are edible nuts, eaten whole and used in many forms. They should never be eaten in large quantities as they contain Prussic acid.

4) How to use saffron (kesar):
This is an orange-coloured spice and should be used sparingly in curries, pilau, sweets and some meat dishes. To make saffron powder: Take 1 tablespoon saffron and $\frac{1}{2}$ tablespoon sugar and grind to a fine powder. Store in an airtight container. Add to recipes as required.

5) Masala paste:
Whenever a recipe calls for masala paste, add only a little water if you need to improve the consistency.

6) Icing sugar:
It is preferable to use icing sugar in decoration of sweets as they 'set' more quickly. It is also easier to decorate sweets using icing sugar.

7) Coconut:
In recipes using creamed coconut, you can substitute with coconut milk. 25 gm. (1 oz.) of creamed coconut is equivalent to half a cup of coconut milk. To make coconut milk: Grate 1 coconut, add 2 cups of water, liquidize and strain. You can substitute desiccated for fresh grated coconut.
Note: It is best to use fresh coconut in curries and pilau, but desiccated coconut will do in sweets.

8) Yoghurt:
Use natural yoghurt in all recipes requiring yoghurt.

9) When making dhokla mixture, or when thinning it, use hot (not boiling) water. The dhokla mixture should be of 'dropping' consistency.

10) Some basic measure conversions (approximate only):
1 tablespoon = 15 ml. (of liquid only)
Tins:
24 x 30 cm. = 9 x 12 in.
15 x 15 cm. = 6 x 6 in.
20 x 20 cm. = 8 x 8 in.
15 x 20 cm. = 6 x 8 in.
18 x 20 cm. = 7 x 8 in.
Cup measures:
1 cup flour = 120 gm. = 4 oz.
1 cup sugar = 250 gm. = 8 oz.
1 cup butter = 150 gm. = 5 oz.
1 cup ghee = 150 gm. = 5 oz.
1 cup golden syrup = 300 gm. = 10 oz.
1 cup chopped nuts = 120 gm. = 4 oz.
1 cup desiccated coconut = 75 gm. = 2½ oz.
1 cup liquid = 8 oz.
2½ cups liquid = 20 oz. or 1 pint
Solid measures:
1 lb. flour = 2 cups
1 lb. icing sugar = 3 cups
1 lb. caster sugar = 2 cups
1 lb. golden syrup = 1 cup
1 lb. dry fruit = 2 cups
½ oz. flour = 1 heaped tablespoon
1 oz. sugar = 1 level tablespoon
½ oz. butter = 1 level tablespoon
1 oz. golden syrup = 1 tablespoon

PART IV	GLOSSARY OF TERMS

Advi leaves = available in Indian grocery shops.
Ajma = bishop-weed seed.
Ambli = tamarind.
Asafoetida = a greyish-white powder with a strong flavour. It is obtained from the gum of a fennel-like plant, and is believed to aid digestion. It should be used sparingly.

Basmati = a variety of long grain rice.
Black rock salt = 'Sanchal', normally available in Indian grocery shops. Has a strong smell — use sparingly.

Channa dal = skinned and split chick-peas (small cream coloured).
Channa flour = gram flour.
Chora = black-eyed beans.
Chori = long green vegetables, similar to French beans.
Cinnamon = brownish strips of bark from the cinnamon tree, a small evergreen tree native to Southern India. Paper-thin strips of the bark are peeled off, rolled into small sticks and dried. Used in puddings, curries, rice, cakes and biscuits, it is delicious in chocolate drinks. It is one of the spices contained in curry powder.
Cloves = small cross-shaped spice. They are best known for their pungent and aromatic flavour. They can be bought whole or powdered, and are used in curries, pickle and rice.
Cocum = mangosteen.
Coriander leaves = green leaves resembling parsley. They give off a strong flavour, particularly when fresh, and are often known as 'Indian parsley'. They are used in most curries.
Cumin seeds = small long pointed seeds, which can be white or black in colour. They can be used whole or ground, and are normally used in conjunction with coriander seeds.
Cup = a normal-sized teacup.

Dhana = coriander seeds. These are small, pale and round. They can be used whole or ground.
Dhana-jeera = a powder mixture of cumin and coriander seeds.

Elaichi = cardamom seeds. Sweet refreshing flavour, commonly used in sweets.
Elcho = large black cardamom pods.

Fennel = small pointed seeds used in cooking.
Flat parsley = green herb, very popular in European cooking.
Fudina = mint.

Garam masala = a mixture of ground cinnamon and cloves (see Part 2 of appendix).
Ghau = whole wheat.
Ghee = melted butter (see Part 2 of appendix).
Gundas = A green round vegetable available in Indian grocery shops.

Haldar = turmeric.
Haricot beans = known as 'white haricot' — the original beans used in baked beans.
Hing = asafoetida.

Jaldalu = dry hunza apricot.
Javantri = mace. This is the musk around the nutmeg kernel. It is orange-brown in colour, with a delicate flavour and is used in sweets.
Jayphal = nutmeg.
Jeera = cumin seed powder.
Jiru = cumin seeds.
Javar or 'Joovar' = wholegrain

Kachories = stuffed pastry balls.
Kadhi = a hot yoghurt soup.
Kand = root vegetable, brownish on the outside and purplish inside, available from Indian grocery shops.
Kesar = saffron.
Kharek = dried dates.
Khus-khus = poppy seeds (small white seeds used in curries and sweets).
Kothmir = coriander leaves.
Kokam = mangosteen.

Lavang = cloves.
Limbdo = curry leaves.

Mange-tout = pale green juicy pods with tiny 'undeveloped' peas inside. To use simply top and tail them.
Masala = mixture — normally spicy for curries.
Masoor dal = split red lentils.
Mava = solidified milk (see Part 2 of appendix).
Methi leaves = fenugreek leaves — green leaves used in Indian cooking. They should be used fresh for flavour in savoury dishes.
Methi seeds = fenugreek seeds — small hard seeds, dull yellow in colour; used either whole or ground.
Mung dal = skinned and split mung beans (or moong).
Mustard seeds = small round black seeds, which may be used whole or ground.

Nutmeg = the fruit of an evergreen tree. The nutmeg spice is extracted after a long drying process. Whole nutmegs are dark brown. Nutmeg is easy to grate and has a delicate flavour, especially when freshly grated. It is used in sweets, vegetables, milk puddings and fruit cakes.

Pakoras = flour balls.
Paneer = chhanno — a type of Indian cottage cheese (see Part 2 of appendix) for method to make.
Papdi = a variety of string beans, dark green in colour with large beans inside.

Parwar = Oval green vegetable available in Indian grocery shop.
Pawa = puffed rice.
Pilau = same as pilaff.

Rajma = kidney beans — maroon in colour, mainly used in Mexican dishes.

Sakaria = sweet potatoes.
Samosa = Indian sweet or savoury in a triangular shape, consisting of an outer pastry shell and a sweet or savoury stuffing.
Saragva sing = long green stick-like vegetable.
Shah-jeera = caraway seeds. Look like cumin seeds and can be used in pilau and curries.
Suran = root vegetable, light peach in colour and available in most Indian grocery shops.

Taj = cinnamon.
Taar = consistency of syrup (see Part 2 of appendix).
Tamal patra = bay leaves. They are normally sold dry and are used in curries.
Thali = a large round steel plate (approx 20 cm. in diameter, used in Indian cooking).
Til seeds = sesame seeds — very small seeds used in curries. They are an excellent source of oil.
Tindoras = available in Indian grocery shops.
Toovar = green beans.
Toovar dal = split yellow lentils.
Turiya = available in Indian grocery shops.
Turmeric = bright yellow spice, predominantly available in powder form. It is used in all curries. It is also a good antiseptic for cuts and wounds.

Urad dal = skinned and split black bean.

Vaghaar = hot seasoning.
Valor = a vegetable similar to green beans, available in Indian grocery shops.

Sweet 'House': *see p. 32*

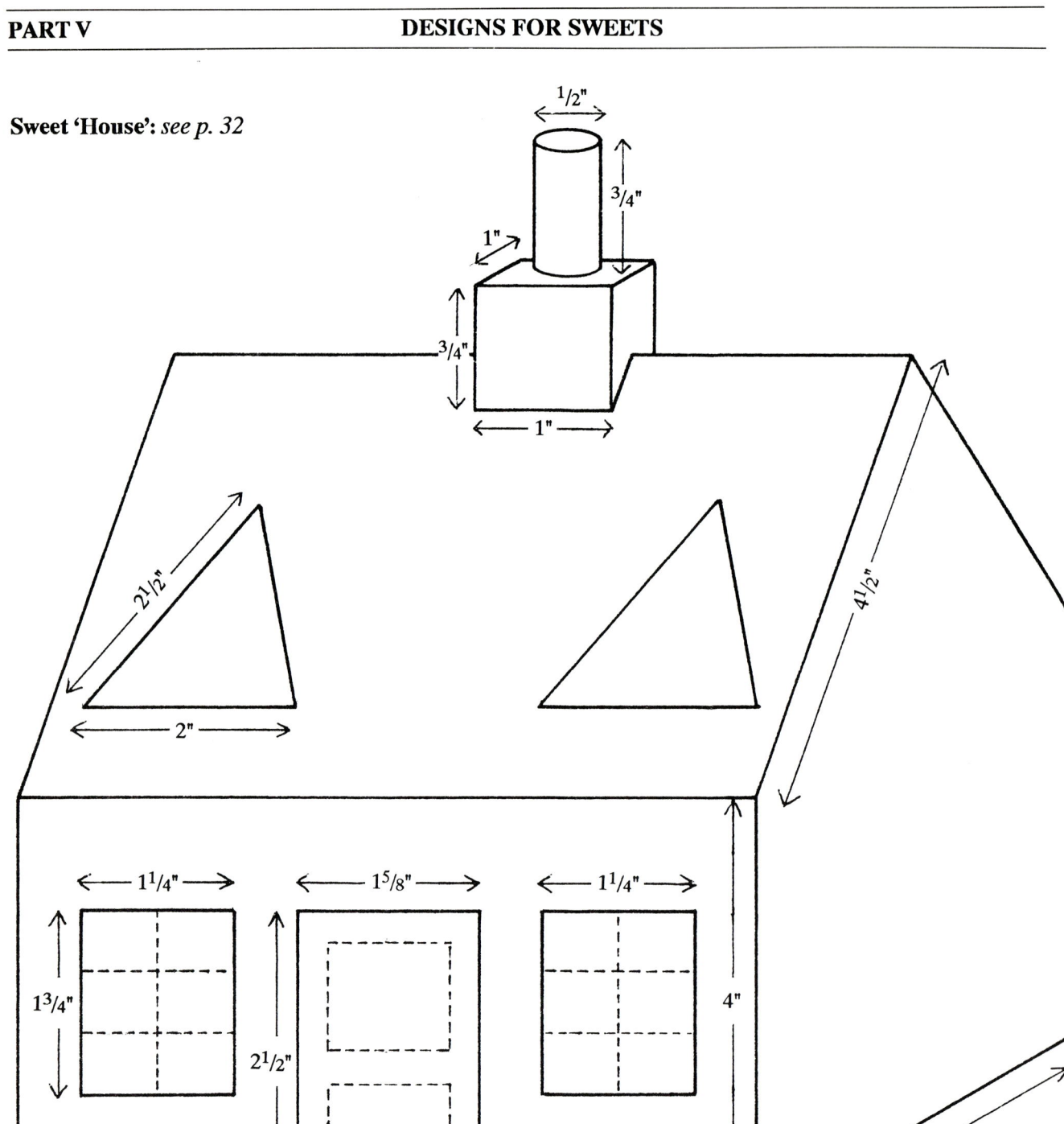

Sunflower Sweet: *see p.28*

Bandhani Sweet: *see p.11*

Peacock Sweet: *see p.9*

INDEX

Cakes and Sweets

Breads

Dals & Kadhis

Bhatiya Kadhi 72

Dal 52

Kadhi 65

Mango Kadhi 48
Moghlai Dal 81
Mung Dal 59

Navratna Kadhi 62

Pakoda Kadhi 75
Panchkuti Dal 68

Shahi Dal 88
Sindhi Kadhi 90

Curry

Aubergines in Gravy 61

Badshahi Vegetables 58
Baked dish 51

Cauliflower Curry 77
Corn Curry 56
Cream Ball Curry 89

Dhansak 45

French Bean Curry in Coconut
Milk 92

Green Granary Kofta Curry 50
Green Kofta Curry 79
Green Peas, Potato & Mange-
Tout Curry 86
Green Stuffed Vegetable Curry 53
Green Tooriya Curry 67
Green Toovar in Coconut Milk 89

Jacket Potato Curry 52

Kofta Curry 46

Mange-tout and Kofta Curry 84
Mange-tout Curry 84
Mixed Vegetable Curry 72
Moghlai Potato Curry 63

Paneer Curry 77
Paneer and Pea Curry 60
Paneer and Pea Curry (Mattar
Paneer) 60
Parsi Curry 45
Potato Curry in Corn Sauce 80
Potato Curry with Green Chutney 74
Potato and Nut Curry 87
Potatoes in Coconut Milk 83
Punjabi Potato Curry 66

Royal Dam Aloo 92

Surti Undhyu 70
Surti Undhuyu 70

Rice

Amiri Pulao 49

Biryani 78
Brinjal & Toovar Pulao 65
Brown Rice 46

Chutney Rice 56

Coconut Rice 63
Corn Rice 91

Spanish Rice 85
Stuffed Rice 79

Tomato Rice 53
Three-in-one Rice 82